The Language and Thought Series

Series Editors
Jerrold J. Katz
D. Terence Langendoen
George A. Miller

Readings in Philosophy of Psychology
Ned Block, Editor

Surface Structure:
The Interface of Autonomous Components
Robert Fiengo

Semantics:
Theories of Meaning in Generative Grammar
Janet Dean Fodor

The Language of Thought
Jerry A. Fodor

Propositional Structure and Illocutionary Force
Jerrold J. Katz

An Integrated Theory of Linguistic Ability
Thomas Bever, Jerrold J. Katz,
and D. Terence Langendoen, Editors
(Distributed by Harper & Row, Publishers)

SURFACE STRUCTURE

The Interface of Autonomous Components

Robert Fiengo

Harvard University Press
Cambridge, Massachusetts
and London, England
1980

Library of Congress Cataloging in Publication Data

Fiengo, Robert, 1949–
  Surface structure.

  (The Language and thought series)
  Bibliography: p.
  Includes index.
  1. Generative grammar. 2. Surface structure
(Linguistics) I. Title.
P158.F5   415   80-14680
ISBN 0-674-85725-9

Acknowledgments

Much of the content of this book reflects the influence of others. Most generally, it is one expression of the theoretical framework developed by Noam Chomsky, as well as an elaboration of some specific proposals of his. Many of the analyses this book contains have been sharpened in conversations with James Higginbotham, Howard Lasnik, Robert May, and Gary Milsark, whose criticisms have been particularly honest and direct. The suggestions of Ed Battistella and Neil Elliott are also incorporated here. The analysis contained in Chapter 3 was begun over ten years ago in a course taught by John Kimball. I regret that I cannot now show to him the result of that first effort.

Contents

With respect to the mind, considered as a complicated apparatus which is to be studied, we are not even so well off as those would be who had to examine and decide upon the mechanism of a watch, merely by observation of the functions of the hands, without being allowed to see the inside. A mechanician, to whom a watch was presented for the first time, would be able to give a good guess as to its structure, from his knowledge of other pieces of contrivance. As soon as he had examined the law of the motion of the hands, he might conceivably invent an instrument with similar properties, in fifty different ways. But in the case of the mind, we have manifestations only, without the smallest power of reference to other similar things, or the least knowledge of structure or process, other than what may be derived from those manifestations. It is the problem of the watch to those who have never seen any mechanism at all.

—De Morgan

1

Introduction

It has sometimes been held that science aims at certainty, and, given this as a goal, two distinct paths have been followed. One path places reliance on objective observation alone, decrying any hypothesis not "grounded" in observation of the external world as subjective, unverifiable, or meaningless. Another path is the "natural gift of reason"; in this view, introspection is the only window to entities untainted by the imperfections characteristic of the observed world and relations holding with perfect regularity. The first path sometimes relies on inductive method as justification for the generalizations it advances; the second, in its strongest forms, rejects empirical inquiry altogether, holding that revelation, not observation, is the key to knowledge of nature.[1] It is fortunate that the paths to certainty are not the only ones open to empirical inquiry, since they are not without their difficulties.

There are alternative conceptions. In some domains it has been found to be possible to construct a formal theory, a set of formal statements, each of which is relevant to the domain that the formal theory is constructed to explain. These statements may be subjected to logical derivations, which make explicit various of the theory's implications, and these implications may be tested against observation. The results of these tests bear on far more than the truth of the observation statements themselves, however, for the tests may show the inadequacies of the entire theory, or may in part confirm it.

Yet this program, which characterizes the practice of much of theoretical science, seems to have strayed from the path to certainty. Although the calculations of the implications of a formal theory may be performed with mathematical precision, the correspondence of those implications to the relevant observation statements is not assured. Furthermore, in the event that a particular theory is found inadequate, there seems to be no automatic procedure, within this conception, for replacing it with a more adequate one. Thus the burden rests squarely on human creativity and critical ability to advance our scientific understanding, and the possibility of achieving certainty comes into question. Yet the situation is not a melancholy one, since progress can and has been achieved.

Now if one attempts to witness with an analytic perspective the progress of a complex event, say an argument between two persons, one is often forced to distinguish between various aspects of it. Perhaps, for example, we observe that the argument is heated. If so, the explanation for its tenor might lie in the importance or urgency of the issue being debated and the fact that the positions are diametrically opposed. Or possibly the argument is really trivial in substance, being merely an excuse for the airing of long, and perhaps silent, personal frustrations. Other explanations and relations between such factors can, of course, be easily imagined. But by isolating such factors one can sometimes come to at least a partial analysis of an event.

As one teases apart the various parameters, one is sometimes enabled to refer to specific disciplines, whose general findings might aid in description and perhaps even in explanation. Studies in the psychology of personality and behavior might, for example, be able at least to describe a particular antipathy, but might offer no explanation for why it should surface at one particular moment instead of some other. It is to be expected that the imperfect and incomplete states of the various disciplines will leave many areas shrouded in mystery, and it seems likely that some domains are intrinsically impervious to scientific investigation.[2] We might know, however, that some of the aspects of the event we are considering could be characterized in terms of more general scientific problems. Thus the analysis of the event might be divided up insofar as the various facets are relevant to programs of research, the complex interaction of phenomena becoming more understandable as the solutions to the problems posed become more refined.

In the study of human language, the problem of finding the identities and interrelationships of the various intersecting parameters is an acute one, for, taking human language in its natural setting, it seems clear that complex and subtle biological and cultural parameters are constantly at play.

Given this, two quite distinct programs of research might be proposed if one were faced with the task of analyzing such a complex system. One might imagine, for example, that an appropriate research procedure would be to begin by dividing the phenomenon into classes of data, requiring that an explanatory theory be constructed for each domain. To take a specific example, consider the analysis of the perception of the speech signal. One might a priori divide the investigation into two domains—the data in one involving such notions as "perceived order of phonetic segments," "perceived sameness or difference of phonetic segments," and so on, the other involving such notions as "rate of perception of phonetic segments," "errors in perceiving phonetic segments," and so on, insisting that separate theories be constructed for the two domains so defined. Similarly, one might divide the class of phonological rules into subdomains (for example, nasalization rules, velarization rules, epenthesis rules, and so forth) and insist that the initial delimitation is in some sense "natural," that is, not itself subject to empirical disconfirmation. Those who adopt such points of view are essentially students of one or more *subject matters,* who, incidentally, often develop a sense of "turf," resenting intrusion by students of other areas.

In an alternative conception, the investigator is a student of one or more *problems,* for example: "How is it possible for a human being to learn a language?" "How is it possible for a human being to process a speech signal?" "Why does the ability of human beings to learn a second language appear to decay across time?" and so forth. The investigator, when following such a program, will place no a priori limitation on what domain data bearing on the question come from, although he might advance as an *empirical hypothesis* the claim that certain theories are autonomous from each other.[3]

The proponent of the first alternative must bear the burden of justifying the initial, a priori delimitation of a domain, whereas the proponent of the second must justify the selection of the problem chosen.

Dogmatic insistence on the first program reduces to the claim that the initial separation of data is "correct" in some absolute sense, a claim that would be miraculous, if true, since the history of scientific inquiry has been consistently marked by change in this very regard. Data that are now productively analyzed within theories of genetics and biochemistry were once grist for the vitalist mill. Theories relating the stars to our day-to-day activities, buttressed by a wealth of observations including star charts and personal histories, have in some circles been replaced by a more justified, if less embracing, point of view. It seems reasonable to assume, then, that unless and until the type of burden alluded to is met, we must search for those interesting questions that are subject to empirical investigation and allow progress in our understanding. As progress is made in answering questions posed, and further, as more refined questions are derived, we can expect that the data base relevant to the solutions will alter. It is in light of this tendency that we can feel confident that the separation of data into domains is an empirical matter itself, not an appropriate topic for dogmatic insistence.

To consider a practical situation, suppose that one places

a strict limitation on the data base, defining a domain, and, having done so, that one also proposes a set of problems that are limited in their scope to the domain defined. It would seem that insofar as progress is gained in answering those questions, the initial delimitation of data is harmless and may be retained. But if such progress is not observed, or if it comes to a halt, it would seem only rational to ask on the one hand whether the initial delimitation of data was the most productive one available, and, on the other, whether the problems chosen might not be improved. An empirical attitude toward such a situation would seem to require that change be possible at both levels. Thus the uncertainty of theoretical science appears to include as much the delimitation of the data base as the "truth" of the theories itself.

As noted, as one theory is replaced by another, so too may the data that are relevant be changed. This is often recognized in a circumstance in which one theory is held to be better than another because it explains all of the data explained by the previous one and more; however, not all theory choices need rely on this type of justification. It may develop, for example, that given a theory of a class of data, there is an alternative conception in which a "split" is effected, the result being that two theories, each with its associated data, arise. The evaluation of whether the split is preferable need not hinge on whether more is explained; it might, rather, involve the relative testability of the systems before and after the split, the naturalness of the idealizations that are made, the uniformity of the primitives of the theories, and so on. The debate, for example, between proponents of "generative semantics" and "interpretive semantics" involved, in part, the question of whether syntactic and semantic investigation should be pursued as autonomous studies, or merged into a single "homogeneous" study.[4]

Admitting that rational change and progress are possible in the pursuit of the answers one seeks, the possibility presents itself that there are limitations on what scientific inquiry can discover.

It is conceivable that, although the genetically conditioned acquisition of tacit knowledge is highly constrained, there are no such boundaries on the conscious human understanding—that scientific understanding is potentially limitless. Yet the alternative, that the human species, in part, owes the acuity of its science-forming abilities, the depth of its scientific outlook, to the narrowness of the questions that it is equipped to pursue, seems a much more realistic outlook. The answers to some questions will forever be shrouded in mystery, in this view, while others will continue to deepen. To return to the problem with which this chapter began, that of analyzing an argument, it would appear that one of the facets of an argument that can be isolated is the possibility that the argument will progress— that the positions will continue to be refined. Since the types of problems that can be successfully approached within this distinctively human form of critical cooperation have so far seemed rather limited, the empirical hypothesis that the areas of mystery will continue to be vast seems quite plausible.[5]

On the Scope of the Problem

Though one can seriously doubt that there could be any a priori justification for limiting the range of data relevant to the construction of a theory, one may, with justification, advance as an empirical hypothesis the claim that certain theories are autonomous from each other. As François Jacob stresses, even so fundamental an analytic distinction as that between synchronic and diachronic description is not intrinsic to the general domain of inquiry, but rather is a distinction to be valued because of its explanatory convenience:

By isolating systems of different kinds and complexity, it is possible to recognize their constituents and justify their relationships. Yet whatever the level studied—molecules, cells, organisms or populations—the perspective is necessarily historical and the principle of explanation necessarily that of succession. Each living system has to be analyzed on two planes, two cross-sections, one horizontal and the other vertical, *which can be separated only for the sake of explanatory convenience.* On the one hand, one has to distinguish the principles governing the integration of organisms, their construction, their functioning; and on the other, the principles that directed their transformations and their succession. The description of a living system requires reference to the logic of its organization as well as to the logic of its evolution. (Jacob, 1973, p. 300; emphasis added)

Taking as our level of inquiry the cognitive capacity of the human species, we may ask, following Jacob, two sorts of questions, one involving the principles that constitute its synchronic organization, the other involving the evolutionary path along which it developed. Although it appears that we know far less about the latter than the former, the questions seem logically to be of equal importance. Though one might decide to pursue one question while ignoring the other, the decision would be one of tactics, not of principle.

Imagine that at some point far in the future we have reached the stage at which we have a synchronic description of the cognitive capacities of many of the species, as well as a refined understanding of the logic of their evolution. Imagine in particular that we have attained an understanding of the material bases of these cognitive capacities, as well as the relation of these material bases to their evolutionary histories.

We would, at that point, be in an enviable position. We would be able to distinguish, for example, those physical structures that are similar in different species because of common inheritance (irrespective of the different uses to which they might be put), that is, the *homologous* structures, from the *analogous* structures which, although evolutionarily distinct, have, nevertheless, a certain similarity based on adaptation to the same function. We would, in short, be able to pursue some of the tasks of comparative biology, and given this orientation, there are certain mistakes that we would not be prone to make.

We would not, for example, conclude from the fact that certain nonhuman primates can be trained to use and understand a communication system accessible to humans that the communicative abilities of human and nonhuman primates are homologous. Furthermore, it would be questionable whether the abilities were even analogous if we found, for example, that the communication system trained to the nonhuman primate was a finite state language, given our knowledge of the synchronic theory of human ability.

We would expect to find qualitative differences between structures agreed to be analogous, not homologous, just as we find these differences when we consider the eye of the ocotpus and the eye of the eagle or the human, for example. We would not expect, necessarily, to be able to form a hierarchy, a sort of great chain of being, in which the analogous structures could be compared in their totality along a single dimension, given the distinct evolutionary histories of these structures.

We would not quibble about whether such and such a species has "Language," no matter how profoundly that last word were intoned, unless we could point to some biologically significant definition of this term independent of a particular species, including humans. We would reject anthropocentrism as jejune.[6]

But science has not yet reached this stage, and the mistakes alluded to are still being made. I believe, however, that there is some progress toward this end in linguistic theory.

We find, in the human species, a vast amount of linguistic diversity. Yet given the analytic techniques that have been developed, we are able to see that the diversity is not a random one but falls, rather, within a remarkably narrow and highly structured range. Accordingly, we are enabled to distinguish between the properties that a language has because the language is a human language, and those that are there through the vagaries of historical linguistic change. The material basis of the biologically determined aspects of human language remains to be described in any detail, yet a precise characterization of the human linguistic universals will no doubt aid in that task.

It is remarkable that linguistic theory is able to characterize certain cognitive abilities of the human species as a whole, given the great variation in observed behavior that the species manifests. Yet it is even more remarkable that people working in certain areas of cognitive ability attempt to characterize variation in the species without any general theory of the dimensions within which this variation is supposed to exist. I believe that the thesis that there are genetically based differences in IQ is of this latter type.

Consider as an example the program pursued by Jensen. Taking as data the scores on IQ tests and the race of the subjects, Jensen, through statistical techniques, arrives at the conclusion that there may be a genetically based racial difference in IQ. It is of interest to consider the relation between certain a priori assumptions concerning the data on which the program is based and the scope of the questions that he poses.

To begin, consider Jensen's definition of the central notion "intelligence." Edwin G. Boring's observation that "intelligence, by definition, is what intelligence tests measure" is adopted as the "proper" conception of the notion; the idea that these tests may fall short, may be misguided, and so forth, is dismissed by Jensen as "a misconception" (Jensen, 1972, p. 68). It is, then, this operational definition that Jensen has in mind in this statement of the hypothesis that he defends:

> There is an increasing realization among students of the psychology of the disadvantaged that the discrepancy in their average performance cannot be completely or directly attributed to discrimination or inequalities in education. It seems not unreasonable, in view of the fact that intelligence variation has a large genetic component, to hypothesize that genetic factors may play a part in this picture. But such an hypothesis is anathema to many social scientists. The idea that the lower average intelligence and scholastic performance of Negroes could involve, not only environmental, but also genetic, factors has indeed been strongly denounced (e.g., Pettigrew, 1964). But it has been neither contradicted nor discredited by evidence. (Jensen, 1972, p. 162)

By assuming the operational definition, Jensen appears to believe that he has either solved, or risen above, any problems arising from an empirical analysis of the human cognitive capacity.[7] What he has done, however, is merely to make himself immune, within the premises of his own methodology, from attack stemming from any general theory of mental capacity that differs in its conclusions from those that he advances. If that attack is not based on IQ tests, he can respond that such a theory is not concerned with intelligence (in his sense) and the rest of his position stands.

Suppose that in the quotation above the word "IQ" were substituted for "intelligence," and imagine (what is by no means obvious) that sense could be made of the statement that IQ variation "has a large genetic component." Then the results Jensen presents should be anathema to no one, since they are consistent with the conclusion that IQ is not a measure of intelligence.

The detachment from empirical orientation that an operational definition allows becomes clear when one realizes that from the existence of a particular measuring device M, one cannot infer that "what is measured by M" is anything more than an epiphenomenon.[8] Given a theory of a complex entity E which analyzes E's various components with respect to their properties and relations, it does not follow that an arbitrary measuring device will isolate any significant aspect of it. Thus Jensen's program is not only insured against falsification but also appears irrelevant to any realistic program to determine the nature of the human mental capacity.

The distinction between a program such as Jensen's and the one defended here is in part a question of the scope of the inquiry. Human intelligence, in the normal, nonoperational sense of this term, and human cognitive capacities in general are, at base, properties of the species. While variation no doubt exists, the parameters within which variation is observed might be quite narrowly defined, if we abstract away from gross abnormalities. Although the attempt to quantify "intelligence levels" seems approximately as revealing as attempting to "measure" the beauty of various paintings by counting brush strokes, and almost as replicable, the primary problem with Jensen's program is that it fails to contribute any understanding of the nature of the intelligence of our species, while purporting to explain variation with respect to that construct. One would expect the universal parameters of human intelligence to be subtle and complex, and any serious attempt to "measure" intelligence may be doomed. However such evaluations might be done, it seems clear that their value would depend on the adequacy of the general theory of intelligence that is presupposed.

At one level, then, the scope of linguistic theory is the structure of the cognitive capacities of the species. A creative tension is maintained between proposals derived to explain variations within the species and those derived to define the linguistic ability of the species itself. But by pursuing the inquiry on these two levels, we gain confidence that our definitions of the relevant parameters are not arbitrary ones.

Theories of Linguistics

Taking linguistic theory to be a study whose scope extends to the level of properties of the species as such, the empirical problem of separating those aspects of linguistic knowledge that are genetically determined from those aspects due to environmental factors may be posed. Within the present volume certain assumptions concerning this relationship will be defended, and I wish to make these assumptions explicit at the outset. We may begin by orienting the discussion with respect to the notion "derivation."

On Derivational Constraints

A derivation may be most generally defined as a finite sequence of phrase markers. If every member of a sequence is a phrase marker, the sequence constitutes a logically possible derivation. There are, to be sure, many logically possible derivations that are ruled out by various empirically motivated conditions. In this brief exposition, I wish to call such a condition a "derivational constraint" and to consider what types of derivational constraints there are.

Let us take as our starting point the set of all logically possible derivations. The set will include all of the derivations of all the sentences of all the natural languages, as well as all of the derivations that do not have that status. Let us call this set D. One empirical problem we face is to partition D in such a way that each subset of D whose members are all and only the derivations of a possible natural language is defined as such. Such definitions may be effected by postulating derivational constraints.

The most familiar form of derivational constraint states conditions under which two phrase markers may be adjacent in a derivation. Such derivational constraints are called "local" rules, and are often thought to be rules of particular grammars.

A "global" derivational constraint states conditions under which more than two phrase markers or two nonadjacent phrase markers may appear in a derivation. A rule that must refer to two phrase markers (for example, a "semantic" phrase marker and a "syntactic" phrase marker) as input is a commonly proposed type of global rule.[9] Similarly, a rule-ordering statement is global in that, in order to determine whether it is satisfied, it is necessary to examine more than two adjacent phrase markers.

A filter is a derivational constraint that relates two adjacent phrase markers which may differ from each other only in that one contains * and the other does not. A filter is an obligatory local rule, which assigns * in specified contexts. By their very nature, filters are obligatory context-sensitive rules; an obligatory context-free filter would assign * to all phrase markers.

We might define another type of filter, an applicational filter, which would assign * to a derivation containing the two adjacent, distinct phrase markers PM_i, PM_{i+1} just in case the relation between them had some property P. Suppose we were to appeal to a condition on application such as the Tensed-S Condition of Chomsky (1977c). We might then formalize the Tensed-S Condition as an applicational filter assigning * just in case the relation proscribed by the Tensed-S Condition held between two adjacent phrase markers in a derivation. In this volume, I defend the thesis that there are no applicational filters of this sort, all filters simply assigning * if a single phrase marker has a particular structure.

The question of which of the mechanisms described are universal and which are language-specific is an empirical one. The imposition of universal derivational constraints divides the set D into two subsets d and d', d' being the set of derivations ruled out on universal grounds and d being the remainder. The imposition of language-particular derivational constraints divides the set d into the subsets d_a, d_b, d_c, and so on, in such a way that each d_i is the set of all and only the derivations of a particular language L_i. Again, the conditions that divide D into d and d' may be filters, local derivational constraints, or global ones; the same obtains for those conditions that divide d into d_a, d_b, d_c, and so on. To take a position within this range of possibilities is to make an empirical claim.

I will defend the position here that there are no language-particular global derivational constraints. Thus I make the claim that d may be partitioned into d_a, d_b, d_c, and so on, by reference to local derivational constraints and filters, but not global rules. The motivation for making this claim rests, of course, on the observation that if, in the postulation of grammatical analyses, a wider range of grammatical rules is available, the "space" from which analyses may be selected is thereby increased and the definition of those cognitive structures that the species may acquire is weakened. By constructing a metatheory that limits the class of principles that may be appealed to in linguistic description in empirically motivated ways, the goal of linguistic theory is thereby advanced.

Turning now to the relation between the separable domains of syntax and the rules interpreting syntactic descriptions, which I will term "semantics," it will be of use to describe three theories of the structural relation between them in terms of the derivations that they allow. I have in mind the Standard, Extended Standard, and Revised Extended Standard Theories.[10]

On the Standard, Extended Standard, and
Revised Extended Standard Theories

While the three linguistic theories mentioned embody
distinct theories of the relation between syntax and semantics, it is also true that particular formulations of these
theories, and particular grammars that conform to the requirements they impose, may differ, as a result, in many
other ways as well. It will be best, then, to enter this brief
discussion by abstracting away from such differences and
focusing solely on derivational structure.

We will begin this overview with some simplifying assumptions. Let us assume, given a set d_i, that every member
of d_i is of the form:

$$(. \ . \ . \ , PM_i, \ . \ . \ . \ , PM_n, \ . \ . \ .)$$

where all rules relating PM_j to PM_{j+1} ($i \leq j \leq n$) are either
syntactic rules or semantic rules. Let us further assume that
there are no rules relating PM_k to PM_{k+1} ($k < i$ or $k \geq n$)
that are syntactic or semantic rules. This assumption
amounts to the stipulation that there is, within any derivation, a continuous subdomain $(PM_i, \ . \ . \ . \ , PM_n)$ in which
all of the syntactic and semantic properties and relations of
a sentence are represented.

A further simplifying assumption will be that all syntactic
and semantic rules are local. There are, as mentioned above,
other logical possibilities, but (except where indicated
below) these possibilities simply add complications irrelevant to the points being made here.

Given these assumptions, we may distinguish between
Standard Theory (ST), Extended Standard Theory (EST), and
Revised Extended Standard Theory (REST) as follows. Ac-
cording to ST, all derivations have the form:

$$(. \ . \ . \ , PM_i, \ . \ . \ . \ , PM_s, \ . \ . \ . \ , PM_n, \ . \ . \ .)$$

where all rules that apply in the continuous subdomain
$(PM_i, \ . \ . \ . \ , PM_s)$ are semantic rules, and all rules that apply in the continuous subdomain $(PM_s, \ . \ . \ . \ , PM_n)$ are
syntactic rules. PM_s is both generated by a phrase structure
grammar and is the point at which lexical insertion applies.

It is referred to as the deep structure phrase marker of the derivation;[11] PM_n is the surface structure; and PM_i is the semantic representation.

Derivations generated by a grammar as defined by EST have the form:

$$(. \ . \ . \ , PM_i, \ . \ . \ . \ , PM_s, \ . \ . \ . \ , PM_n, \ . \ . \ . \ , PM_p, \ . \ . \ .)$$

where all rules that apply in the continuous subdomains $(PM_i, \ . \ . \ . \ , PM_s)$ and $(PM_n, \ . \ . \ . \ , PM_p)$ are semantic rules,[12] and all rules that apply in the continuous subdomain $(PM_s, \ . \ . \ . \ , PM_n)$ are syntactic, as before. This theory has interesting implications for the representations of semantic information.

Assume, for example, that we require, as a derivational constraint, that every well-formed derivation contain a single phrase marker, in which is represented all of the semantic properties and relations of the sentence whose derivation it is. Since, within EST, "semantic information" will be derived in both the subdomains $(PM_i, \ . \ . \ . \ , PM_s)$ and $(PM_n, \ . \ . \ . \ , PM_p)$, it follows that there must be at least one rule that relates a structure in one domain to a structure in the other. This rule (or rules) might, for example, copy semantic information derived in one subdomain into the other in order that the entire semantic representation be derived.

Now note that this observation alone does not entail that any grammar that conforms to the principles of EST must contain a language-particular global derivational constraint. It is logically and empirically possible that such a rule (or rules) would be universal and stated in the metatheory, not in any particular grammar. Imagine, however, for the sake of argument, that there is motivation for the conclusion that there are such language-particular global derivational constraints, assuming, as we have, that we require of each derivation that it contain a single phrase marker that constitutes the entire semantic representation of the sentence. This would, of course, violate the metatheoretical assumptions assumed here; it would not necessarily increase the class of possible grammars, however.

Whether the inclusion of language-particular global constraints increases the class of possible grammars or not depends on the nature of the metatheory. If the metatheory states simply that grammars may contain local or global rules *ad libitum*, then the class of grammars is increased. If, however, the metatheory requires that particular rules (for example, rules that apply at a particular point in the derivation) *must* be formalized as global, and if, furthermore, the input to the global rules is fixed metatheoretically, the class of grammars would not thereby be increased. In this metatheory, grammars that contained local rules that applied at the designated point in the derivation would be disallowed. Similarly, grammars that *lacked* these global rules would be disallowed. It might well be that grammars that contained the required global rules would be evaluated as more complex than grammars that were in all other respects identical, but used only local rules. But the issue then is simplicity, not restrictiveness.[13]

According to REST, all derivations have the form:

$$(. \ldots, PM_i, \ldots, PM_n, \ldots, PM_p, \ldots)$$

where all rules that apply in the subdomain $(PM_i, \ldots, PM_n)$ are syntactic rules, all rules that apply in the subdomain $(PM_n, \ldots, PM_p)$ are semantic rules, and PM_n is the surface structure. In the present volume it is this last metatheory that is defended. Before outlining this theory in more detail, it will be worthwhile to consider an example of an empirical argument that leads to the conclusion that at least some of the information necessary to semantic interpretation should be derived from surface structure.

Consider a grammar in which the assumptions are made that the reciprocal pronoun "each other" is present in deep structure, that the transformation of NP-Movement is available, and that there is a rule, RR, which determines the antecedent of the reciprocal pronoun.[14]

It would appear that this last must be a semantic rule, at least in the broad sense, since it refers to semantic properties of the antecedent expression, or at least that the output of this rule must itself be input to semantic interpretation, as we will see.

Given these assumptions, consider underlying structures such as those in (1) and (2).

(1) The policemen believed [the demonstrators to have harassed each other]

(2) The policemen believed [the demonstrators to have been harassed each other by Δ]

(1) yields (3), and (2) yields (4) by NP-Movement; the italics indicate an anaphoric relation.

(3) The policemen believed *the demonstrators* to have harassed *each other*

(4) *The policemen* believed *each other* to have been harassed by the demonstrators

These derivations are to be contrasted with ones that have deep structures such as in (5) and (6) and yield (7) and (8), respectively.

(5) The policemen believed [each other to have harassed the demonstrators]

(6) The policemen believed [each other to have been harassed the demonstrators by Δ]

(7) *The policemen* believed *each other* to have harassed the demonstrators

(8) The policemen believed *the demonstrators* to have been harassed by *each other*

A simple generalization unites (3), (4), (7), and (8); the *NP* immediately preceding *each other* is the antecedent.[15] Stating the generalization at the level of deep structure is a significantly more complicated task; the following statements embrace the cases at hand:

(9) The matrix subject (*the policemen*) is the antecedent of *each other* just in case:
  (a) *each other* is subject and the embedded VP does not contain *by* Δ
  (b) *each other* is object and the embedded VP does contain *by* Δ

(10) The embedded subject (*the demonstrators*) is the antecedent of *each other* just in case:

(a) *each other* is object and the embedded VP does not contain *by* Δ

Note further that the passive construction is not itself the source of the complexity. A complexity similar in kind (but different in source) arises in the derivations that have (11) and (12) as deep structures, and (13) and (14) as surface structures:

(11) Δ seems to each other [the men to love the women]

(12) Δ seems to each other [the men to be loved the women by Δ]

(13) *The men* seem to *each other* to love the women

(14) *The women* seem to *each other* to be loved by the men

These examples, and many others like them, suggest that the restriction that anaphora rules, and in particular, RR, apply at deep structure, as ST would seem to require, serves only to complicate the grammar. The pairs (3), (4); (7), (8); and (13), (14) appear to differ greatly in truth conditions; though the members of each pair have some semantic similarities, they appear to express quite different propositions. That these differences are the result of an anaphora rule, whose simplest formulation requires application at surface structure, indicates the motivation for the claim that surface structure contributes to semantic interpretation directly.

In the chapters that follow, a sustained argument will be made to the effect that surface structure is the *only* level that undergoes semantic interpretation. The theory of grammar whose implications I will consider allows derivations of the following form:

(15)

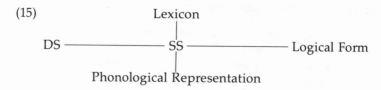

There are, then, four rule systems in this conception, each of which relates to the level of surface structure.

The derivational structure in (15) is part of a proposed solution to the question of what the levels of description in a linguistic analysis are. The attempt is made to separate the set of rules into components and to specify distinct conditions on membership for the rules in each. In this sense, the components are autonomous. Each component, it will be argued, has one or more core rules,[16] each of which is an unmarked variant, a maximally simple statement, of a class of rules allowed by linguistic theory. We thereby gain the desired tension between the goal of determining the properties of language universal to the species and the goal of describing the variation within the species, since, as will be seen, the unmarked variant of a rule must often be supplemented if the variation observed is to be described. Prominent in this supplementation will be the filters. As the study of the various components deepens, the structure of their interface, surface structure, will emerge.

2

Movement and Hopping

The notion of surface structure as developed in this volume is a level of representation, a set of structures, whose form depends solely on the nature of the rules, both grammar-particular and universal, which are postulated in the construction of this particular theory. While this point may seem obvious, I wish to stress the implications of this view, since it means that the notion of surface structure (or any other level) derived here is not a pretheoretic one, but rather one derived in the course of empirical investigation. The notion of surface sturcture presented in this volume, or, to speak extensionally, the class of structures that comprise that level, is not equivalent to the level postulated in any other generative account of English as far as I know. Therefore, it would perhaps be less misleading to select a new name for this level; however, I intend to retain it, since the level postulated does have some of the conceptually more central properties of surface structure as conceived of in other theories. It is, however, distinct from many other theories in that it constitutes the level of lexical insertion as well as the input to the component that determines the syntax of logical form. It is like other theories in that it constitutes the output of the transformational component, but again it should be stressed that the content of the transformational component will be quite minimal as presented here, containing only rules such as "Move *wh*," "Move NP," and "Move PP," as will be seen. Thus surface structure as developed here stands at the nexus of no less than four rule systems:

(1)

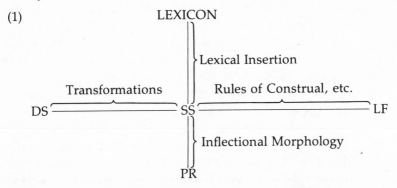

LEXICON

Lexical Insertion

Transformations   Rules of Construal, etc.

DS ———————————— SS ———————————— LF

Inflectional Morphology

PR

This being the case, a few comments are in order concerning the methodological considerations involved in determining the appropriate interaction of two or more "tangent" components.

To see what is involved, in my opinion, it is useful to begin by considering a class C, which is the set of structures at the interface of two or more derivational processes. (2) is an illustration:

(2)

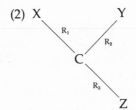

X R_1 Y R_2 C R_3 Z

where X, Y, Z, . . . constitute other levels, and R_1, R_2, R_3, . . . are the rule systems relating X, Y, Z, . . . to C. Let us say that, due to the form and functioning of rules R_1, R_2, R_3, only representations C', C", C"', are allowed at the level C. It is clear that if a sentence is to be grammatical, there must be a member of the intersection of the sets C',

C", C'", such that it constitutes the representation of that sentence at C. Given this conception, we may now pose our original question somewhat more precisely.

Consider some generalization g which might be formalized as r_1, a rule in R_1, or as r_2, a rule in R_2. Let us assume that the two options are equivalent in the sense that one theory generates the levels C', X', Y', Z', . . . , while the other theory generates the levels C", X", Y", Z", . . . , where the membership of C' is roughly equivalent to the membership of C", the membership of X' is roughly equivalent to the membership of X", and so forth. Assuming this, how does one choose between the two theories?

There has been no lack of manifestos issued on this topic. Consider, for example, the position of Anderson:[1] "There is an obvious advantage to making the subclass of lexical redundancy rules as large as possible. Wherever a transformation can be equally well reformulated as a lexical relation, the number of steps between underlying and surface structure is reduced, along with the degree of abstractness of the former. The approximation of underlying to (independently observable) surface structures thus follow from Occam's razor, again assuming that lexical and transformational formulations are descriptively equivalent" (Anderson, 1977, p. 364). This position seems to be implicit in much recent work; it is difficult to find any methodological grounds for its attractiveness, however.

Let us first point out that a simplicity metric such as Occam's razor measures the simplicity of a *theory*. A derivation (or set of these) is not a theory. It is a grammar, rather, which may be thought of as a theory of a language, and there are circumstances, as is well known, in which a simplification in a grammar results in an increase in the length of derivations that the grammar generates. The most trivial of examples will suffice. Consider the passive construction, and imagine two rules, (3a) and (3b), which, for purposes of discussion, we will imagine are descriptively equivalent.

(3) (a) X NP   Y   V NP Z
         1   2   3   4   5   6
         1   5   3 be+en 4   ∅   6   by 2
    (b) move NP

One difference between (3a) and (3b) is that in the derivation of the passive construction, (3a) only has to apply once, whereas there are two applications of (3b) that are required. What chooses between these theories? Do we hold the possibly greater "abstractness" of the underlying structures generated by a grammar including (3b) against that rule? Do we do so even though that rule is *formally* simpler than (3a)? Do we do so even if rule (3b) happens to constitute a (partial) description of properties of *other* constructions? If the simplicity of theories (grammars) is our goal, the answer to these questions is, manifestly, no.

Let us consider the word "abstract" in more detail. Intuition presents several distinct senses of this word to the mind. Imagine a theory so constructed that there are a small number of simple axiomatic principles from which, perhaps through quite complex logical deductions, quite specific and detailed empirical predictions can be derived. We might call the axiomatic principles "abstract" in that they are the furthest removed in the deductive structure of the theory from the statements of these predictions themselves, while admiring the compactness and simplicity of the theory so constructed. In such theories, simplicity and abstractness are jointly exemplified.

In another sense of abstractness, reference is made to unobservable entities which theories posit to exist. It is sometimes claimed that a theory should posit as few abstract entities as possible, the remainder being "concrete," with a close relation being held to exist between "what is concrete" and "what is observable." I believe Anderson uses the term "abstract" in this sense, although a central component of this conception, an account of what the class of observable entities is in the study of language, appears to be absent.

While "abstractness" in the first sense of the term may be considered a desirable property of a theory, it would seem premature to place a methodological evaluation on the term in its second sense. I should add that this second sense has a connotation in which abstract entities are thought to be uncertain, vague, or inexplicit, concrete ones being certain, clear, and explicit. I assume all would agree that no theory should posit abstract entities in this sense.

Let us now consider the tension between the transformational component and the lexicon as competing loci of the explanation of phenomena. Although such a topic becomes quite complex in the context of detailed empirical investigation of natural languages, certain general aspects of the situation are easy to grasp.

Let us say we have a situation, as Anderson proposes, in which there are two descriptively equivalent formulations of a generalization, one transformational, the other lexical. Clearly, if we have a grammar in which the generalization is stated transformationally and replace it with another grammar in which the relevant transformation is removed and the lexical component enriched, we have a trade-off. This trade-off can be justified as a principled one on various grounds, among them the following: (1) if the formal simplicity metric can evaluate the relative simplicity of the lexical rule and the transformation, the simpler will obviously be more highly valued, and (2) on the metatheoretical level, if one formulation allows a more restrictive theory of the form of rules than the other, its adoption will be more highly valued. To give an example, suppose that the transformational formulation, say, requires that the class of syntactic primitives be increased in order to accommodate it, whereas the lexical formulation does not require that the descriptive power of the lexical component be increased. In this circumstance, the grammar with the lexical formulation would be consistent with a more restrictive theory of (the primitives of) syntactic description while the richness of the lexical descriptive apparatus would not be increased, and, for this reason, would be a better choice. It is clear that (1) and (2) above could come into conflict, and, I should emphasize, they are not exclusive. The conflict between them, which would occur in a situation in which the most restrictive metatheory increases the complexity of description, is to be expected, however; it is one of the familiar tensions between the goals of explanation and description.

Returning now to Anderson's position, we notice that these considerations play no role. The criterion of minimizing "abstractness" is absolute. But, more specifically, there appears to be the implicit assumption that the "abstractness" of structures in *lexical* derivations is either so slight as to be negligible or is not itself subject to the same principles of evaluation as transformational derivations. Yet no hint is given as to why we should believe this. Thus we are face to face with an a prioristic evaluation, without any empirical analysis or philosophical argument that might make the evaluation plausible, or any metatheoretical argumentation that might justify it.

We may now return to one of the points made at the beginning of this section by noting that Anderson's conception of surface structure is a pretheoretic one—in fact, Anderson considers surface structures "independently [independent of what?] observable." I find this very hard to imagine, given the properties of any of the notions of surface structure that have so far been proposed. In none of the theories so far constructed is that level phonetically interpreted, for example. Recalling, furthermore, that in every formulation of generative grammar so far devised the level of surface structure is comprised of *phrase markers*, the likelihood of their being "observed" diminishes. For they are not data; their structure is an empirical question, concerning which sensible people can, and have, disagreed. Such disagreement involves competing grammatical formulations which yield distinct descriptions at that level, not quarrels concerning "observed" structural properties. At least so it seems to me.

The views expressed by Anderson reflect, in part, the position of Bresnan. In a paper published in 1978, Bresnan presents the "lexical-interpretive theory of transformational grammar," one of the central tenets of which is that the lexical component should be enriched so as to incorporate generalizations expressed transformationally in EST. In her words:

Schematic as this overview has been, it allows a basic idea to be expressed very simply: As nontransformational relations are factored out of the transformational component, the transformational complexity of sentences is reduced, deep structures more closely resemble surface structures, and the grammar becomes more easily realized within an adequate model of language use.

The next section will show how this idea suggested by the lexical-interpretive model can be radically extended to yield a more realistic model of transformational grammar. But let us first anticipate a possible objection.

"Clearly," the objection runs, "if you eliminate a lot of transformations, you may get a more efficient syntactic processing system, but the greater efficiency of one component is purchased by a greater inefficiency of the other components. So it is hard to see why the model as a whole will be more realistic."

In answer to this objection, I must make explicit several assumptions. First, I assume that the syntactic and semantic components of a grammar should correspond psychologically to an active, automatic processing system that makes use of a very limited short-term memory. This accords with the assumptions of Chapter 3. Second, I assume that the pragmatic procedures for producing and understanding language in context belong to an inferential system that makes use of long-term memory and general knowledge. The extreme rapidity of language comprehension then suggests that we should minimize the information that requires grammatical processing and maximize the information that permits inferential interpretation. Finally, I assume that it is easier for us to look something up than it is to compute it. It does in fact appear that our lexical capacity— the long-term capability to remember lexical information—is very large. (Bresnan, 1978, p. 14)

These assumptions are to be viewed within the context of Bresnan's general conception of grammatical realism:

A realistic grammar must be not only psychologically real in this [Levelt's] broad sense, but also realizable. That is, we should be able to define for it explicit realization mappings to psychological models of language use. These realizations should map distinct grammatical rules and units into distinct processing operations and informational units in such a way that different rule types of the grammar are associated with different processing functions. If distinct grammatical rules were not distinguished in a psychological model under some realization mapping, the grammatical distinctions would not be "realized" in any form psychologically, and the grammar could not be said to represent the knowledge of the language user in any psychologically interesting sense (Bresnan, 1978, p. 3)

Bresnan points to the ATN (Augmented Transition Network) system as one possible realization of the lexical-interpretive theory, noting that each component of a grammar, be it phrase structural, lexical, or functional, constructed within this theory "can correspond to separate components of an ATN system," in conformity to the view of realism she presents. *Ceteris paribus,* other computer systems in which on-line processing is dear and memory cheap will be a possible realization of a grammar constructed along lexical-interpretive lines.

It is not only with respect to the size of the lexical component she proposes that Bresnan finds a realization correspondence to ATN. The fact that ATN contains a phrase structure parser that makes only minimal use of the kinds of generalizations captured by transformations suggests, given Bresnan's view of realism, that the transformational component of grammars should be correspondingly small. She accepts, as we would expect, the conclusion of much research in psycholinguistics that while grammatical structures are psychologically real, grammatical transformations are not.

It should be clear to the reader that the specific analytic proposals of lexical-interpretive grammar and the conception of realism Bresnan presents can be detached from each other. One might, in principle, find the lexical-interpretive analysis of the passive construction convincing but reject her view of realism. More interestingly, one could accept her view of realism and reject lexical-interpretive theory. I myself accept neither, but I will restrict myself here to arguing that no appeal to realism in Bresnan's sense can inform us, given our present understanding, as to what the appropriate division of labor is among the various components of grammars of natural languages, leaving the discussion of lexical-interpretive theory for another occasion.

The first question I wish to raise concerns the relevance of computer systems in general to the construction of theories of human language. Imagine a grammar constructed in such a way that it has a rich and complex syntactic component and a lexical component that is minimal. Is such a grammar "realizable" (in Bresnan's sense) in some *existing* computer system? Depending on the sorts of relations expressed in the grammar, the answer might be no. But from this it does not follow that *no* computer system could "realize" the grammar imagined. Since we clearly do not want our theories of the cognitive capacities of humans to be dictated by the present state of the art in computer technology (which depends for its progress on economic considerations independent of work in the human cognitive domain), we can gain, apparently, no insight into the correctness of a particular theoretical proposal in linguistic theory from such analogies. If we could appeal to principles of such strength that they would preclude the realization of the proposed theory in *any* physical system (including the human brain), however constructed, given any level of technological development, an argument of the desired sort might be constructed. I know of no interesting principles of this latter sort. Consequently, I deny the relevance of "realizability" in *existing* computer systems to choice between theories of grammar.

The problem of determining the "realization" relation between knowledge of language, as expressed within linguistic theory, and its psychological or material basis, as expressed by psychological or neuropsychological theory, would be best addressed by erecting the best theory of each without making a priori assumptions concerning what the relation between them should be. In particular, I see no reason to assume that each rule of a particular grammar must correspond to a distinct processing operation. More generally, I see little sense in arguing *whether* a particular theoretical construct is realized in the absence of debate concerning *how* such a construct might be realized.

We might distinguish between three empirical inquiries: linguistics, psychology, and neurophysics. Thought of as theoretical sciences, it appears that they have proceeded in such a way that distinct classes of data fall under each of them. In the case of linguistics, we have judgments concerning sentences of various languages; in the case of psychology, we have data such as reaction times, perceived categorical distinctness, and so on; and in the case of neurophysics, we have data concerning the physical structure of the brain. Any theory that makes an empirical claim concerning how these three autonomous inquiries should be related—any theory, for example, that posits "bridge laws" to relate them—should be applauded as a step toward establishing the "reality" of the theories involved. However, I see little reason to believe, and no point in claiming, that linguistic theory "matches" either psychological or neurophysical theory, given their distinct data bases.

Consider, in this light, two English-speaking populations, one human, one Martian. Imagine that the two populations are, for all intents and purposes, identical with respect to their reported linguistic intuitions, but that their reaction times, brain structures, and so on, are distinct. This would be the familiar circumstance in which two distinct physical systems possess the same ability.

Now as traditionally conceived, one theory of competence in English would account for the observed behavior of the two populations, which would be indiscriminable with respect to the data on which that theory would be based. But according to Bresnan, the grammar constructed would not represent the knowledge of at least one of the populations "in any psychologically interesting sense," since the mental processes, reaction times, and so forth of at least one of the populations will not correspond to the rules of the grammar constructed. We infer that, according to Bresnan, the only way something of "psychological interest" could be gained in the description of these two populations would be if *two* grammars were constructed, each of them realizable in her sense.

What does Bresnan mean by "psychological interest?" Does she mean that if a grammar is not a model of mental processes, it has no utility at all? This view is surely unacceptable as a condition on theories of psychology. Suppose, to select an example from the domain of visual perception, we wish to test the hypothesis that the obscurity of an image is a depth cue.[2] Must we possess a model of the visual system in which that hypothesis (which might be formalized in a variety of ways) is *realized* (in Bresnan's sense) before we acknowledge the utility of the hypothesis? Surely not. Thus we conclude that Bresnan cannot maintain that traditional conceptions of psychological reality lack utility. The traditional conception will, for example, distinguish the human and Martian populations, on the one hand, from (say) the giraffe, which lacks competence in English, on the other.

Is it a problem for the traditional conception of competence that it will not distinguish between the human and Martian populations? The answer to this question is no. Distinguishing between knowledge as represented by grammars based on intuitions concerning sentences and psychological (or physical) theories of processing, we would wish to maintain that the human and Martian populations have the same knowledge, effected by distinct mechanisms. However, since Bresnan denies that the grammar that humans and Martians share has "any psychological interest," the identity between their knowledge is not accounted for.

Let us end this digression by considering the assumptions that buttress Bresnan's argument. Since they are without support, it is sufficient to deny them explicitly. Consider the assumption that "the syntactic and semantic components of the grammar should correspond psychologically to an active, automatic processing system that makes use of a very limited short-term memory." Since "a very limited short-term memory" might be best described by a quite complex algorithm, this assumption is of no direct relevance to the division of labor among the components of a grammar. We have here three entities—a memory, an algorithm, and a grammar—but Bresnan gives us no reason to believe that, by some miracle, these converge in size in the optimal general account.

As for the assumption that it is easier for humans to look something up than it is to compute it, which is tied to the alleged fact that "our lexical capacity—the long-term capability to remember lexical information—is very large," we ask, if this is Bresnan's assumption, what is her thesis? We would have thought that the "size" of our capacities (whatever this might mean) is an empirical question, and would ask what sense of "ease" Bresnan assumes.

It is difficult to know exactly what Bresnan has in mind in

these statements, but it smacks of the sort of psychologism that led many to believe, for example, that if the derivational theory of complexity were not confirmed for a particular transformational grammar, that grammar would not be psychologically real. But this point of view must be rejected as an assumption. Had transformational grammars passed the test set by the derivational theory of complexity experiments, we would have been witness to a miracle—the one-to-one correspondence of inferred mental processes to the statements of a formal theory constructed on totally independent data. Though miracles may happen, we resist basing theories on the assumption that they have.

In the present chapter, I will at several points consider the interaction of syntactic and lexical description, and a few specific proposals will be developed in Chapter 3. As a final remark, I hope I have made it clear to the reader that I consider the nature of this interaction in a balanced way; the antisyntactic bias of Anderson's and Bresnan's remarks seems to me to be the very antithesis of an empirical attitude on this question. Before we begin, however, it is necessary to make a few remarks concerning the notion "core grammar."

Some Remarks on the Notion "Movement"

As stated in my previous works (Fiengo, 1974, 1977), I assume that movement of an element leaves a "trace" in the position from which movement occurs. To take a particular case, I assume that movement of NP_i to position NP_j (where A and B are the contents of these nodes) in (4) yields (5) as a derived constituent structure, where NP_i/e is the trace of NP_i/B.

$$(4) \ldots NP_j \ldots NP_i \ldots$$
$$| \qquad |$$
$$A \qquad B$$

$$(5) \ldots NP_i \ldots NP_i \ldots$$
$$| \qquad |$$
$$B \qquad e$$

(6) Move NP

I furthermore wish to develop the implications of the hypothesis that (6) is the rule of NP-Movement in English (see Chomsky, 1977d). The formulation in (6) states, implicitly, that movement may be either to the left or the right.

This is a distinct proposal from that made in my paper "On Trace Theory" (Fiengo, 1977), in which I argued that there are two distinct rules, NP-Preposing and NP-Postposing, which apply in the derivations of sentential and nominal passives as well as raising constructions. I claimed in that article that in order to derive a nominal such as (7), it is necessary to postulate an underlying structure such as (8), an intermediate structure derived by NP-Postposing as in (9), and a "Spelling Rule" (as well as *of*-Insertion) to yield (10).[3]

(7) the destruction of Carthage by Rome

(8) Rome$_i$ destruction Carthage$_j$ by Δ

(9) [$_{NP_i}$ e] destruction Carthage$_j$ by Rome$_i$

(10) the destruction of Carthage$_j$ by Rome$_i$

The existence of a rule of NP-Postposing has been questioned, however. Hornstein, who assumes the general theory outlined in my 1977 paper, makes the following comment: "It is interesting to note that a trace theory without spelling rules would predict that no rightward NP movement rules exist. This would significantly limit the types of possible transformations and by weakening the formal power of the theory would strengthen its explanatory adequacy. Trace theory, with this modification, would become, among other things, a condition on the formal properties of transformational rules" (Hornstein, 1977, p. 147). In response, I wish to distinguish two notions: rightward movement applications and rightward movement rules. One can, to make the distinction obvious, affirm the existence of the former without affirming the existence of the latter; this is, in fact, the stand I wish to take in this volume. If one accepts that (6) is the formulation of the NP-Movement transformation in English, it would clearly be a step backward to enrich the theory with the stipulation that movement is only to the left. From this point of view, the stipulation that NP-Movement is only to the left would clearly not "limit the types of possible transformations." Allowing such a minimal formulation of NP-Movement is obviously not without its dangers; the task of limiting overgeneration by appeal to properties of other components is complex. As the reader will see, however, the task is not an impossible one.

I also follow Chomsky (1977e) in assuming that the formulation "move *wh*" is adequate as a statement of the *wh*-Movement rule in English.

Some Remarks on the Notion "Core Grammar"

With Chomsky (1977e, 1978), I assume that "universal grammar provides a highly restricted system of 'core grammar,' which represents in effect the 'unmarked case.'" The language learner, beginning with this optimal system, will be confronted with the task of learning various idiosyncratic constructions at the periphery, for which richer descriptive devices will be needed. These will be the marked constructions of the language.

In Chomsky and Lasnik (1978), core grammar is assigned the following structure:

(11)

1. Base rules
2. Transformational rules

3a. Deletion rules	3b. Construal rules
4a. Filters	4b. Interpretive rules
5a. Phonology and stylistic rules	5b. Conditions on binding

I assume, with Chomsky, that the rule system (1) is highly constrained by the X-bar theory.[4] I am, furthermore, in sympathy with the proposal of Chomsky (1978) that the content of (2) can be restricted to the rule "Move α," where α is a category whose identity will be considered; however, I will not attempt to develop all the implications of this view, nor the (virtually) equivalent view that empty categories are generated in (1), and that there is no rule "Move α" (see the section on PRO and trace in Chapter 4). I do not, however, hold that there are deletion rules (3a) or filters on complementizer constructions (4a). This last difference between the theory of grammar as stated in Chomsky and Lasnik (1977) and Chomsky (1978) as against my own is developed in Chapter 3.

In this chapter, I will explore the hypothesis that the class of rules that have traditionally been called syntactic rules can and should be partitioned into two classes, one class consisting of the rule "Move α," which covers applications of NP-Movement and *wh*-Movement (as well as, perhaps, PP-Movement; see the section on the Specificity Condition in Chapter 4), and the other class consisting of the local rule "Hop C," where C is a grammatical formative, and "hop" a local operation in a sense that will be defined. The rule "Hop C" subsumes, in my system, such traditional rules as Affix Hopping, Subject-Aux Inversion, Particle Movement, and perhaps Q-Floating. These last rules have a morphological flavor; I consider the rule "Hop C" to be the core movement rule of inflectional morphology.

It is my thesis that "Move α" may be restricted in its application to the movement of phrasal categories and that "Hop C" may be restricted in its application to the movement of the grammatical formatives. The autonomy of the two components thus consists in part in the disjointness of the elements which their core rules may affect. It will be the major task of this chapter to argue that while "Move α" relates DS and SS, "Hop C" applies between SS and PR. Given a derivational structure as in (12), it follows that while LF (and SR) are determined in part by application of the rule "Move α," Hop C has no such effect.

(12)

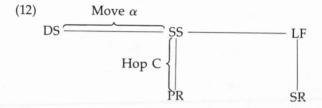

On the Feature ±Affect in
the Description of English

Passive and Semipassive Nominalizations

Given a rule of the generality of "Move NP," we find, as would be expected, that the rule "overgenerates," that is to say, while surface structures of the form (13a) and (13b) may be syntactically well formed, they may violate other conditions in the grammar; for example, they may not correspond to a well-formed morphological representation, or again, they may not correspond to a well-formed logical form.

$$(13) \quad (a) \quad \ldots \text{NP}_i \ldots e_i \ldots$$
$$(b) \quad \ldots e_i \ldots \text{NP}_i \ldots$$

Given the orientation adopted here that conditions on application are in principle excluded (apart from the specification of a primitive operation and the element that this affects —that is, the maximally simple statement of a rule itself), it follows that such cases of overgeneration must be eliminated by conditions on membership at various levels (that is, filters). The common desiderata of simplicity and generality are, of course, as relevant to the postulation of filters as they are to any proposed generalization in any formal theory.

Furthermore, as the generality of any proposed generalization increases, and the "distance" from the data, as measured by the complexity of the deductive structure of the theory, increases, the potential for focusing in on the universal parameters of the theory as a whole becomes greater. This is as true of theories that rely on filters as it is of theories that do not. It would seem to me to be premature and possibly quite misguided to insist that all filters be universal in scope and all rules grammar-particular, or vice versa. More motivated, it would seem, would be a program that set as its task to identify the universal parameters of each, aiming always for generality. In any event, it should be clear that filters, looked at in this way, are neither more nor less ad hoc in principle than any other linguistic formalism.

Let us now focus on cases of overgeneration of the form (14):

$$(14) \ldots NP_i \ldots e_i \ldots$$

The first set of cases that I wish to consider are illustrated in the (a) members of the following triplets:

(15) (a) *great relief's expression by John
    (b) the expression of great relief by John
    (c) Great relief was expressed by John

(16) (a) *some money's gift to the library by John
    (b) the gift of some money to the library by John
    (c) Some money was given to the library by John

(17) (a) *irregularities' acknowledgment by the senators
    (b) the acknowledgment of irregularities by the senators
    (c) Irregularities were acknowledged by the senators

(18) (a) *the charge's denial by the defendant
    (b) the denial of the charge by the defendant
    (c) The charge was denied by the defendant

(19) (a) *the government's perception by the media
    (b) the perception of the government by the media
    (c) The government was perceived (as corrupt) by the media

These examples illustrate the overgeneration of NP-Movement in nominals. The (b) examples show that, in other respects, the nominals are possible, and the (c) examples show that the sentential passive is allowed. Any filter designed to rule out the (a) examples, then, must not apply to the (c) examples, which are also of the form (14). Furthermore, the (a) examples must be distinguished from those in (20) through (24), where the preposing of the NP is apparently allowed:

(20) Carthage's destruction by Rome

(21) the product's distribution by the owners

(22) the movement's infiltration by spies

(23) the prisoner's execution by the authorities

(24) the proposal's alteration by the authors

Establishing a principled explanation for the contrast between the (a) examples of (15) through (19) and (20) through (24) would appear to be a more difficult task than distinguishing (15a) through (19a) from (15c) through (19c), since there are several structural distinctions that might be exploited in the latter case, whereas in the former case the examples are structurally identical.

Focusing, then, on the harder problem, we note that those nominalizations that contain objects that are *unaffected* seem to disallow the preposed structure.[5] This notion, if it can be made precise, is a semantical one; it does not depend on syntactical shape alone (since, for example, (15a) and (20) are identical in this regard) but rather depends on the interpretation of words in these structures. As a preliminary formalization of the relevant principle, consider (25):

(25) Given the structure:
 . . . NP_i's N e_i . . .
interpret NP_i as [+affect]

Let us note first of all that, considering (26) and (27), we wish to express the fact that the object of the verb in the first is changed by the action of destroying, whereas in the second the action of the verb "express" does not alter its object.

(26) Rome destroyed Carthage

(27) John expressed great relief

The "do-to" construction seems to select only those predicates that require affected objects:

(28) What Rome did to Carthage was destroy it

(29) *What John did to great relief was express it

It is important to note that this property of predicates appears to be independent of (though related to) whether the predicates express activities (as opposed to states); both (30) and (31) are allowed, whereas (32), in which the predicate expresses a state, is disallowed.

(30) What Rome did was destroy Carthage

(31) What John did was express great relief

(32) *What John did was know algebra

All affected objects are related to active verbs, but not vice versa. It appears to be the notion [±affect], not [±active], which is operating in the NP-Movement cases discussed so far.

Along with rule (25), we allow ourselves the statement given in (33), which I believe corresponds to a quite clear intuition concerning the items involved:

(33) The object of the class of nouns $N_{[-AF]}$ is [−affect], where $N_{[-AF]}$ = {expression, gift, acknowledgment, denial, perception, knowledge, . . .}

The statements (25) and (33) will come into conflict as they apply to a structure such as (34):

(34) . . . $[_{NP_i}$ serenity's] expression $[_{NP_i}$ e] . . .

While (25) will require that the interpreted object be [+affect], (33) will contradict this, as desired. An example such as (35) will be allowed, however, since "destruction" does not belong to $N_{[-AF]}$.

(35) . . . $[_{NP_i}$ Rome's] destruction $[_{NP_i}$ e] . . .

We will return later to the question of the status of (25) and (33).

Let us now broaden our investigation of the internal structure of NPs to include the distribution of *by*-phrases. As we will see, the notion "affect" plays a role here as well.

Consider the pair in (36):

(36) (a) the Buddha's expression of serenity
    (b) the expression of serenity by the Buddha

The pair differ in that (36b) can only refer to an active expression of serenity, the chanting of a mantra, for example, whereas (36a) allows reference to a passive as well as active expression. For example, (36a) can refer to the expression on the statue of the Buddha, whereas (36b) cannot. The contrast between (37) and (38) illustrates the same point.

(37) (a) a linguist's definition of the term
     (b) a dictionary's definition of the term

(38) (a) the definition of the term by a linguist
     (b) *the definition of the term by a dictionary

While one may speak of a linguist constructing, postulating (and so on) definitions, dictionaries do not perform such activities. Other such contrasts, which can be multiplied at will, include the following:

(39) (a) the suggestion of a different tactic by John
     (b) *the suggestion of depth by the painting

(40) (a) the perfection of the mechanism by the scientist
     (b) *the perfection of technique by John

(41) (a) the description of the house by the author
     (b) *the description of the house by the book

In order to make the appropriate distinction, it would seem to be sufficient to require that *by*-phrases in NPs contain agents, where we take agents in the broad sense as the doers of actions, whether intentional or unintentional.[6] Yet it would seem more parsimonious to use the feature [±affect] for subjects as well; corresponding to affected objects, we will have affector subjects, to put it crudely, which are generally referred to as agents.

It is to be stressed that if this point of view is adopted, the notion "agent" is not to be viewed as an unanalyzed primitive within a system of thematic relations, as is often thought, but rather as a complex notion composed of the feature [+affect] and the subject designation.[7] Conversely, any system that makes use of the notion "agent" covertly makes use of the notion "affect," it would appear.

Returning to the problem at hand, we now have two subgeneralizations to consider: on the one hand, preposed objects in NPs must be [+affect]; on the other, *by*-phrases in NPs must contain NPs that are [+affect]. We are seeking a theory that will incorporate these two.

It is my belief that an appeal to the Case system in NPs can yield a parsimonious characterization of some of these phenomena. We must first, however, consider those mechanisms that assign Case in NPs.[8]

As a preliminary theory of Case assignment in NPs, I propose the following. We first notice that only two Case forms are distinguished in NPs, the Possessive and the Oblique. Of particular interest to us is that the Possessive appears on NPs in SPEC; the NP objects of prepositions are in general Oblique, with the notable apparent exception of such constructions as "a friend of John's," which are not directly relevant to the issue at hand. We are free, then, to postulate the binary opposition [±oblique], where [+oblique] is assigned, roughly as in Chomsky (1978), by the following mechanism:

(42) NP is [+oblique] when governed by P(reposition) or V(erb)

We adopt the notion of government given in Chomsky (1978):

(43) α is *governed* by β if α is c-commanded by β and no major category or major category boundary appears between α and β[9]

This allows us to distinguish between (44a) and (44b):

(44) (a) the destruction of it
     (b) *the destruction of its

The Possessive Case will be [−oblique] in the NP system. If, however, the syntactic environment that determines Possessive Case is SPEC, we cannot maintain that all Case assignment derives from government, in Chomsky's sense. In (45), the NP "his" is not governed by SPEC, since SPEC, because it contains the NP, does not c-command the NP (see note 9).

(45) $[_{NP}[_{SPEC}[_{NP}\ his]]\ hat]$

Speculating, I propose that the assignment of [−oblique]

Case depends not on government but on "determination," which I provisionally define as follows:

(46) α is *determined* by β if α is immediately dominated by β

The desired generalization is now as follows:

(47) NP is [−oblique] when determined by SPEC

This allows us to distinguish (48a) and (48b):

(48) (a) its destruction
     (b) *it destruction

To digress for a moment, it is interesting to note that this system extends rather naturally to the sentential system. Departing from Chomsky (1978), let us suppose that the Case system in both NPs and Ss is [±oblique], with [−oblique] being realized as Possessive in NPs and Nominative in S. Suppose further that Nominative depends not on Tense but on the complementizer *that* (or its allomorphs—see Chapter 3) for its assignment.[10] Suppose finally that we extend determination in the following way:

(49) α is determined by β if α is immediately dominated by β or if β is the sister of γ and α is immediately dominated by γ

Analyzing COMP as the SPEC of S, we may reformulate (47) as (50):

(50) NP is [−oblique] when determined by:
     (i) SPEC of NP
     (ii) SPEC$_{+THAT}$ of S

It is stipulated in (50ii) that the SPEC be SPEC$_{+THAT}$ since the FOR complementizer assigns [+oblique] Case, as sentences such as "for him to leave would be awful" attest. As will be argued in Chapter 3, the two allomorphs *that* and $\emptyset$ of the morpheme THAT may appear in SPEC$_{+THAT}$, as well as the *wh*-words, and, in these positions, Nominative Case is assigned. Only the two allomorphs of FOR, *for* and $\emptyset$, assign [+oblique]. (Here and in the previous sentence, members of the morphemic level are capitalized and their allomorphic variants italicized.) These questions of execution will be presented in Chapter 3 in more detail. As a final point, we note as a benefit of the system constructed here that it allows the assignment of Nominative in "subjunctive" complements, which lack Tense:

(51) I demand that he leave

Turning now to the question of where in the derivation Case is assigned, it appears that assignment at the level of SS is the only realistic alternative, given that it must follow NP-Movement but precede the application of certain principles that apply at LF. Consequently, we assume that SS is the level of Case assignment. An entailment of this is that *wh*-words inherit the Case assigned to their traces; this mechanism will explain the contrast in (52):[11]

(52) $\begin{Bmatrix} \text{Who} \\ \text{*Whom} \end{Bmatrix}$ do you think was more intelligent

I also assume that the (semantical) opposition [±subject] is assigned at the level of SS, perhaps along the lines suggested in my article on trace theory (Fiengo, 1977). It should be emphasized that the notion "subject" being considered is not the syntactical notion "NP immediately dominated by S," which is made use of in the Specified Subject Condition, for example. "Sincerity" will be [+sub] in both "sincerity frightens John" and "John is frightened by sincerity" in my use of the term.

Consider an NP such as (53), given this theory of Case and subject:

(53) Rome's destruction of Carthage

Given the system developed, we have the following representation:

(54) $\begin{bmatrix} -\text{Obl} \\ +\text{Sub} \end{bmatrix}$ Rome's] destruction $\begin{bmatrix} +\text{Obl} \\ -\text{Sub} \end{bmatrix}$ Carthage]

Consider now the NP (55):

(55) Carthage's destruction by Rome

(55) is to be represented as follows:

(56) $\begin{bmatrix} -\text{Obl} \\ -\text{Sub} \end{bmatrix}$ Carthage's] destruction by $\begin{bmatrix} +\text{Obl} \\ +\text{Sub} \end{bmatrix}$ Rome]

Let us now postulate the following rule, which we will for the moment assume applies only in nominals:

(57)
$$\emptyset \rightarrow +\text{Affect} \; / \; \begin{bmatrix} \overline{} \\ \alpha\text{Oblique} \\ \alpha\text{Subject} \end{bmatrix}$$

Given this system, we may now return to the examples that motivated this digression.

Consider first (15a):

(15) (a) *great relief's expression by John

(15a) will have the representation (58):

(58) $\begin{bmatrix} +\text{Aff} \\ -\text{Obl} \\ -\text{Sub} \end{bmatrix}$ great relief's] expression by $\begin{bmatrix} +\text{Aff} \\ +\text{Obl} \\ +\text{Sub} \end{bmatrix}$ John]

The rule assigning the feature [+affect] will, of course, be inapplicable to the NP "great relief" in (59):

(59) the expression of $\begin{bmatrix} +\text{Obl} \\ -\text{Sub} \end{bmatrix}$ great relief]

by $\begin{bmatrix} +\text{Aff} \\ +\text{Sub} \\ +\text{Obl} \end{bmatrix}$ John]

Given such representations, it will follow that (58) is well formed only if "expression" can be interpreted as having an affected object. But it cannot; "expression" belongs to $N_{[-\text{AF}]}$.

An example such as (38b), repeated here, behaves similarly:

(38) (b) *the definition of the term by a dictionary

(38b) will have the representation:

$$(60) \text{ the definition of } \begin{bmatrix} +\text{Obl} \\ -\text{Sub} \end{bmatrix} \text{ the term}]$$

$$\text{by } \begin{bmatrix} +\text{Aff} \\ +\text{Obl} \\ +\text{Sub} \end{bmatrix} \text{ a dictionary}]$$

Although "definition" can take [+affect] subjects, as in "the definition of the term by a linguist," it seems clear that "dictionary" cannot be interpreted as the affector of a definition, and we again have the desired contradiction.

We assume that there is another list, similar to that in (33), which states which nouns have [+affect] subjects. We will return to this point directly.

Assuming the generalizations to express correctly the possible positions of NPs within derived nominals, it is relevant to consider the analogous structures in gerunds. Gerunds are similar to the derived nominals in that they contain genitives in subject position; they are dissimilar, of course, in that they have the internal structure of Ss.

We note that the gerunds behave, in general, like other Ss with respect to the passive construction:

(61) (a) They resented [that emotion's having been expressed by John]
(b) *They resented [that emotion's expression by John]

(62) (a) They resented [the government's being perceived as corrupt by the media]
(b) *They resented [the government's perception (as corrupt) by the media]

(63) (a) We were aware of [that stock's having been given to the college]
(b) *We were aware of [that stock's gift to the college]

Since we have in the (b) examples of (61) through (63) cases in which a genitive unaffected object is preposed, we draw the conclusion that the generalization expressed in (57) applies in nominals alone.

We may now turn to the question of the status of the lists

we have appealed to, which state for particular nouns whether they may have [+affect] subjects and objects. How should these lists be viewed? Do they express generalizations within the lexicon or are they part of the extragrammatical knowledge captured at SR?

Let us first attempt to characterize some of the relevant data. To begin, the object of a noun is always separated from it by a preposition. We have examples such as (64), but never (65).

(64) Rome's destruction of Carthage

Rome's attack $\left\{ \begin{array}{c} \text{on} \\ \text{*of} \end{array} \right\}$ Carthage

(65) *Rome's destruction Carthage
*Rome's attack Carthage

The reason for this phenomenon will be discussed in the following section.

We note that only objects that are preceded by the preposition "of" in the active nominal may occur preposed in the passive nominal; we have (66), but not (67):

(66) Carthage's destruction by Rome

(67) *Carthage's attack by Rome

Furthermore, of the hundreds of nouns whose objects are preceded by "of," virtually all are deverbal, morphologically related to transitive verbs.

These facts receive an explanation in the following way. Suppose that we have a PS-Rule of the form (68), and a rule of *of*-Insertion as in (69):

(68) $\overline{\text{N}} \rightarrow$ N (NP)(PP) . . .

(69) $\emptyset \rightarrow$ of / . . . N___NP . . .

The PS-Rule is apparently optimal, as it may be collapsed with the rule expanding $\overline{\text{V}}$(VP). The rule of *of*-Insertion has utility outside of the class of cases we are considering (for example, all [of] the men; see Fiengo and Lasnik, 1973). We may now appeal to the proposal of Chomsky (1970) that verbs and their associated nouns may share a single subcategorization statement. The element D, which is realized as either the noun "destruction" or the verb "destroy," depending on the environment, will have the specified syntactic environment (70):

$$(70) \ [\underline{\quad} NP \ . \ . \ .]$$

The noun "attack," on the other hand, will be given the syntactic environment (71), which is distinct from that of its associated verb.

$$(71) \ [\underline{\quad} PP \ . \ . \ .]$$

The noun "attack," as well as "emphasis," "resemblance," "marriage," "resistance," "doubt," "desire," "fight," and a few others, are unusual in that they are related to transitive verbs but take a preposition other than "of' before their objects. The general case is that of "destruction," including over a hundred ending in -(a)*tion*, and scores ending in -*ment*, -*ance*, and -*al*.

It is clear, then, that the lexical regularity is as expressed in (70).

There is, on the other hand, a considerable amount of idiosyncratic variation within the class of nouns with respect to the feature [±affect]. The distinction between (72) and (73) depends on the extragrammatical knowledge that a country can change another country's status by recognizing it, whereas the same is not true of persons:

> (72) Cuba's recognition by the U.S.

> (73) *John's recognition by Fred

The following pairs are similarly idiosyncratic:

> (74) (a) John's possession (by the devil)
> (b) *a lot of money's possession

> (75) (a) the definition of the term by Webster
> (b) *the definition of the term by the dictionary

It seems best, therefore, to treat the syntactic regularity of the nouns considered as lexical, and the notion [±affect] as involved in the construction of the level SR. The lists referred to are to be thought of as expressing extragrammatical knowledge, in this view.

We may now consider certain cases of overgeneration in sentences.

On the Interaction of Case and Anaphoric Indices

As noted above, NP-Movement from PP is disallowed.[12] An example is (76):

(76) *$[_{NP_i}$ John] gave $[_{NP_j}$ Fred] to $[_{NP_j}$ e]

Let us consider the reasons for this in detail.

We assume in accordance with trace theory that each NP is assigned a referential index before movement applies: (77) would be an underlying structure, assuming movement:

(77) $[_{NP_2}$ John] gave $[_{NP_4}$ e] to $[_{NP_3}$ Fred]

After movement, (78) is derived:

(78) $[_{NP_2}$ John] gave $[_{NP_3}$ Fred] to $[_{NP_3}$ e]

In accordance with the algorithm developed in the preceding section, Case is assigned:

(79) $[_{NP_2}$ John] gave $[_{NP_3}$ Fred] to $[_{NP_3}$ e]
     NOM   OBL   OBL

We may now assign anaphoric indices to the NPs in (79). Following Chomsky (1978), an anaphoric index of an NP is comprised of the referential indices of all of the c-commanding NPs. Two NPs that have the same referential index I will term "anaphorically related." Two NPs, if one of them contains in its anaphoric index the referential index of the other, will be termed "anaphorically distinct." It is a principle of interpretation, which will be discussed in more detail in Chapter 5, and given its initial formulation below, that no two NPs may be both anaphorically related and anaphorically distinct. Departing from Chomsky (1978), I will assign anaphoric indices to all Cased NPs, including traces. Applying this algorithm, we have (80):

(80) $[_{NP_2}$ John] gave $[_{NP_{(3,(2))}}$ Fred] to $[_{NP_{(3,(2,3))}}$ e]
   NOM   OBL   OBL

According to this interpretation, "Fred" is correctly assigned anaphoric distinctness with respect to "John." However, as originally pointed out by May (1978), the interpretation of *e* is a contradictory one. According to the notation, *e* is said to be both anaphorically related to and anaphorically distinct from "Fred," which is clearly an absurdity. Following May, we will call this filter the "i-set-i Filter," which we will state as in (81):

(81) $*$. . . $[_{NP_{(i,(...i...))}}$ X] . . .

Consider now the structure given in (82):

(82) $[_{NP_2}$ John] gave $[_{NP_{(3,(2))}}$ a book] to $[_{NP_{(4,(2,3))}}$ e]
   NOM   OBL   OBL

Structure (82) would arise not through movement, but through a lack of application of lexical insertion to the final NP. This structure is also ruled out, however, since the final NP is not properly bound; it is not c-commanded by an NP with the same referential index. We will state the proper binding condition as follows (see Chapter 5, where this concept is developed further):

(83) $*$. . . $[_{NP_{(i,(...))}}$ e] . . .

   if there is no $[_{NP_{(i,(...))}}$ X] c-commanding $[_{NP_{(i,(...))}}$ e]

The filter given in (83) is actually considerably more general than as stated; this is also discussed in Chapter 5.

Note that it does not matter, with respect to the pattern of explanation appealed to so far, whether the relevant structures were derived by means of movement operations or were, in fact, generated by PS-rules. (80) and (82) exhaust the possibilities; either the *e*-element is coindexed with another NP in the same structure, or it is not. In these structures, both possibilities are precluded.

Consider now a sentence such as (84):

(84) John was arrested

As is clear, a representation as in (85) must be avoided, if the i-set-i Filter is assumed:

(85) $[_{NP_2}$ John] was arrested $[_{NP_{(2,(2))}}$ e]

Consider, in this light, the structure of (84) before the assignment of anaphoric indices:

(86) $[_{NP_2}$ John] was arrested $[_{NP_2}$ e]

Note that the assignment of Case yields (87):

(87) $[_{NP_2}$ John] was arrested $[_{NP_2}$ e]
     NOM

The final NP in (87) is not assigned Case, since "arrested" belongs to the category Adj; it is not a V, as was assumed in some other analyses.[13] Note also that a structure such as (88) poses no problem either, since "destruction," a member of the category N, does not assign Case:

(88) $[_{NP_2}$ Carthage's] destruction $[_{NP_2}$ e]
     GEN

We note further that an example such as *"Carthage's$_i$ attack against e$_{(i,(i))}$" will be ruled out, since the object of the preposition will receive Case, and the consequent assignment of the anaphoric index will violate i-set-i.

Adopting these mechanisms, we reduce in a principled way the overgeneration of NP-Movement. We can now turn to a consideration of the middle construction, which is of interest in this regard.

The Middle and the Causative

The construction that I wish to term the "middle" is exemplified in (89a) through (z).

(89) (a) The book reads easily/well
     (b) Clay tablets decipher with difficulty
     (c) Pine saws well

(d) Clay shapes well
(e) This pipe smokes nicely
(f) Cheap bread dices unevenly
(g) Wool rugs clean well
(h) A person who isn't self-conscious photographs well
(i) Bread refrigerates poorly
(j) Math theses type slowly
(k) Mistakes erase poorly
(l) The gears on his bicycle shift poorly
(m) Good wood waxes well
(n) Children's toys assemble with difficulty
(o) Cheap basketballs dribble poorly
(p) Transformations order neatly
(q) Foreign cars sell (well)
(r) A thick beard shaves with difficulty
(s) Some tennis balls serve better than others
(t) Dark paint covers poorly
(u) Newsprint binds poorly
(v) The bicycle steers well
(w) Granite lifts with difficulty
(x) Problems solve with difficulty
(y) Eggs poach (well)
(z) Example sentences construct with difficulty

Adverbs have an intriguing distribution in the middle. Those predicates that require an adverb in the middle also require an adverb when they stand as participles in attributive position. There are very few exceptions to this rule. The relevant data follow:

(90) (a) *The book reads
          *a read book
          a frequently read book
     (b) ?Clay tablets decipher
          ?a deciphered tablet
          a recently deciphered tablet
     (c) ?Pine saws
          ?a sawed piece of pine
          a well-sawed piece of pine
     (d) ?Clay shapes
          ?sm shaped clay
          sm nicely shaped clay

(e) *This pipe smokes
     *a smoked pipe
     a frequently smoked pipe

(f) Cheap bread slices
     sm sliced bread
     sm evenly sliced bread

(g) *Rugs clean
     *a cleaned rug
     a well-cleaned rug

(h) *People photograph
     *a photographed person
     a frequently photographed person

(i) Bread refrigerates
     sm refrigerated bread
     sm well-refrigerated bread

(j) *Math theses type
     ??a typed math thesis
     a well-typed math thesis

(k) Mistakes erase
     erased mistakes
     poorly erased mistakes

(l) *The gears shift
     *a shifted gear
     the most frequently shifted gears

(m) Good wood waxes
     waxed wood
     carefully waxed wood

(n) ?Children's toys assemble
     ?an assembled toy
     a carefully assembled toy

(o) *Basketballs dribble
     *a dribbled basketball
     a frequently dribbled basketball

(p) Transformations order
     an ordered transformation
     a well-ordered transformation

(q) Cars sell
     a sold car
     a frequently sold car

(r) *Thick beards shave
     *a shaved beard
     a carefully shaved beard

(s)   *Tennis balls serve
       *a served tennis ball
       a well-served tennis ball

(t)   *Dark paint covers
       *sm covered dark paint
       sm well-covered dark paint

(u)   Newsprint binds
       bound newsprint
       well-bound newsprint

(v)   ?The bicycle steers
       ?a steered bicycle
       an easily steered bicycle

(w)   *Granite lifts
       *sm lifted granite
       ?laboriously lifted granite

(x)   *Problems solve
       ??sm solved problems
       sm infrequently solved problems

(y)   Eggs poach
       poached eggs
       well-poached eggs

(z)   *Example sentences construct
       *a constructed example sentence
       a well-constructed example sentence

There is, furthermore, a related construction in which the reflexive appears:

(91) (a) That clay tablet deciphered itself
     (b) Wool rugs clean themselves
     (c) The gears on his bicycle shift themselves
     (d) Good wood waxes itself
     (e) Foreign cars sell themselves
     (f) Simple problems solve themselves

We will consider the last construction first.

Note first that the stress pattern of the examples in (91) is not the one typically assigned to reflexive constructions. The contrast is simply that the pronoun is stressed (in fact, given primary stress) in the examples in (91), whereas this does not in general occur in normal reflexive environments. The data are as in (92) and (93):

(92) (a) Simple problems solve themsélves
     (b) *Simple problems sólve themselves

(93) (a) *They knew themsélves (if not contrastive)
     (b) They knéw themselves

The stressing of the reflexive pronouns in the examples in (91) recalls the fact that the reflexive in the construction exemplified in (94) is also stressed:

(94) (a) John did it himsélf
     (b) *John díd it himself

(95) (a) They finished the job themsélves
     (b) *They finished the jób themselves

The (a) examples in (94) and (95) are to be contrasted with those in (96):

(96) (a) John himsélf did it
     (b) They themsélves finished the job

The examples in (96) carry a reading in which the subject is highlighted as being important in some way; it is the reading that the Latin *ipse*, as in *ipse dixit*, carries. It also carries a reading in which the subject is said to have performed the activity without aid. I believe that the (a) examples of (94) and (95) carry only this second reading.

It is my belief that the examples in (91) can plausibly be said to carry this latter reading as well. This would be to say that in a sentence such as "foreign cars sell themselves," the reflexive is equivalent to an expression like "without aid."

The apparent meaning of this reflexive form suggests the possibility that it is syntactically an adverb. There is, in fact, distributional evidence to this effect. As has been noted in the past, there is a condition prohibiting the occurrence of two manner adverbs in the same S:

(97) (a) *John did it carefully easily
     (b) *They finished the job slowly shrewdly

The generalization seems to be a syntactic one; the examples of (98) are grammatical and presumably carry the meanings that the examples in (97) would carry if they were syntactically well formed.

(98) (a) John did it carefully and easily
(b) They finished the job slowly and shrewdly

Turning now to the stressed reflexive form, we note the same pattern:

(99) (a) *John did it himsélf easily
(b) *They finished the job themsélves shrewdly

(100) (a) *John did it easily himsélf
(b) *They finished the job shrewdly themsélves

And when we consider the middle construction, we find the same pattern:

(101) (a) *Foreign cars sell themsélves easily
(b) *Foreign cars sell easily themsélves

We may now pose the question as to whether in the middle construction we have a structure as in (102) or as in (103):

(102) $[_{NP}$ Foreign cars] sell $[_{NP}$ e] $\begin{Bmatrix} \text{easily} \\ \text{themselves} \end{Bmatrix}$

(103) $[_{NP}$ Foreign cars] sell $\begin{Bmatrix} \text{easily} \\ \text{themselves} \end{Bmatrix}$

If the structure in (102) is assumed, we have a problem. We know that for the structure to be well formed, *e* must carry the same index as the NP "foreign cars." Since *e* is in object position, we would normally assume that it would be assigned Oblique Case. The indexing algorithm will produce (104):

(104) $[_{NP_2}$ Foreign cars] sell $[_{NP_{(2,(2))}}$ e] $\begin{Bmatrix} \text{easily} \\ \text{themselves} \end{Bmatrix}$
NOM   OBL

Yet structure (104) contains the contradictory index and will be designated as ungrammatical by the i-set-i Filter.

On the other hand, if (103) is assumed, we again have a problem: why is "foreign cars" interpreted as the *object* of "sell"? Were (104) well formed, given our assumptions, this would follow from the same mechanism that yields this result for examples such as (105).

(105) $[_{NP_2}$ Foreign cars] were sold $[_{NP_2}$ e]

The basic mechanism is that if an NP has a trace, it is the position of the trace that determines the grammatical relation of the NP.[14]

The problem raised here is not necessarily limited to the middle construction. The so-called causative and its related intransitive are similar:

(106) (a) The bell jangled
(b) John jangled the bell

(107) (a) The sauce thickened
(b) Max thickened the sauce

(108) (a) Her expression changed
(b) Sue changed her expression

The table shown below gives an incomplete, but probably representative, list of the verbs that occur in such pairings.

spill	diminish	increase	loosen	separate
soften	smoothen	lessen	mellow	scatter
sit	redden	disperse	merge	ripen
stand	whiten	ease	moisten	revive
lean	blacken	liven up	change	unite
lie	begin	decrease	flatten	reunite
tilt	stop	inflate	freshen	vibrate
stir	cease	?embolden	awaken	retreat
dissolve	wind up	interlock	warm	advance
melt	commence	mix	(un)tangle	resume
spread	end	?intermix	(un)button	reduce
shatter	accumulate	reverse	unlock	overturn
blow up	improve	jangle	transfer	turn
cool	bend	lessen	toughen	develop
circulate	alter	level	thicken	fry
freeze	blow	topple	?telescope	bake
gather	bleed	lighten	swing	boil
issue	burn	brighten	spin	cook
twist	congeal	stiffen	start	steep
cheapen	corrode	steepen	thaw	broil
devaluate	split	divide	bang	roast
disintegrate	fade	form	simmer	
metamorphose	break	tighten	sharpen	

It is possible to resolve the problem raised by the middle construction, though not necessarily intransitives such as (106a), (107a), and (108a), in such a way that movement is assumed while avoiding the i-set-i Filter. One might stipulate of the class of verbs which occurs in this construction that they, unlike non-middle verbs, do not assign Case. On this analysis, (109) and not (104) would be generated:

(109) $[_{NP_2}$ Foreign cars] sell $[_{NP_2}$ e] $\begin{Bmatrix} \text{easily} \\ \text{themselves} \end{Bmatrix}$

Structure (104) violates the i-set-i Filter, as mentioned before, but (109) does not. A structure such as (110) would be allowed, as desired, but (111) would not be, since we wish to state the general condition that lexical NPs must be assigned Case.[15]

(110) $[_{NP_2}$ John] sells $[_{NP_{(3,(2))}}$ foreign cars]
    NOM   OBL

(111) $[_{NP_2}$ John] sells $[_{NP_3}$ foreign cars]
    NOM

Why is it that members of the class of verbs that occur in the middle construction do not assign Case? The answer to this question appears to lie in the distributional similarities between middle verbs and their morphologically related adjectival forms. As the paradigm (90) attests, middle verbs and their related adjectives are alike in their subcategorization of adverbs. Both the middle verbs and their related adjectives contrast in this respect with verbs not appearing in the middle construction; (112) and (113) are examples of this.

(112) (a) *Tennis balls serve
     (b) *a served tennis ball
     (c) John served a tennis ball

(113) (a) Tennis balls serve well
     (b) a well-served tennis ball
     (c) John served a tennis ball well

The phenomenon may be described simply by stating that middle verbs do not assign Case, since adjectives do not.

In fact, the formal similarity of subcategorization and Case assignment, at least as regards objects, suggests that, at least in a configurational language such as English, the two mechanisms may be collapsed.[16] But I will make no specific technical proposal here.

As a last point, it is of interest to speculate as to why an element that has the shape of a middle verb should acquire the subcategorizational properties of an adjective. In answering this question, it would seem important to bear in mind that the middle construction, though productive within limits, is a marked construction, at least with respect to the active and passive voices. In such a circumstance, the possibility of interaction with properties of SR arises, in particular the possibility that certain properties of the meanings of middle verbs condition their syntactic distribution. That the middle voice in English seems most appropriate in sentences with a generic flavor is suggestive in this regard, since the generic interpretation of a verb that would normally express a specific activity expresses, rather, a general attribute of its subject. That general attributes are, in the unmarked case, expressed by adjectives completes our pattern of reasoning. This proposal, though coherent, remains mere speculation, however, since the parameters being manipulated are not, in general, well understood.

Concerning pairs such as "John spilled the milk" and "the milk spilled," we have the option of treating the regularity as lexical or of allowing "spill" not to assign Case, when apparently intransitive, to its trace object:

$$(114) \quad [_{NP_i} \text{ The milk}] \text{ spilled } [_{NP_i} \text{ e}]$$

One factor that seems to mitigate against a surface structure such as (114) is that in middles and passives there is a subject either stated or implied; in "the car was sold" it is implied that there was an agent of the sale, and in "foreign cars sell easily" the same is true. The sentences "the milk spilled" and "the milk was spilled," or "the tomato ripened" and "the tomato was ripened," seem to contrast in this respect, the "intransitives" implying no agent. In a previous work (Fiengo, 1974) I discussed the alternative analyses of the intransitives, but no conclusion was drawn. I continue to consider this question to be open.

Implications for the Structure of Components

We have seen in the discussion above that in order to attain descriptive adequacy with a grammar that incorporates a maximally simple rule of NP-Movement, it is necessary to appeal to certain features of a clearly nonsyntactic nature. The implications of using such features in the explanation of the properties of NP-Movement constructions becomes clear when the form of derivations allowed in the present theory is considered. Since the outputs of NP-Movement are present at the level of surface structure, it is in principle possible to filter out some of the NP-Movement outputs at the level of LF or SR. Notice, however, that outputs of rules that apply between the levels of SS and PR cannot be filtered at the levels of LF or SR, assuming, as we do, that the metatheory precludes any appeal to global mechanisms in the formulation of linguistic generalizations. In the section that follows, we will consider applications of a rule that "follows" SS and "precedes" PR. It will be seen that the outputs of this rule need not be filtered by any semantical statements. Accordingly, it will be concluded that, by positioning this rule between SS and PR, the metatheory has made the correct partition of the components, since it precludes this possibility.

The rule that I will develop is named "Hop C." Briefly, it is a rule that moves a grammatical formative over one and only one constituent. I will propose that it be included in the class of "core" rules.

I ask the reader to bear in mind that in the various versions of the Standard Theory, the rules of NP-Movement (for example, Passive, Dative, Tough-Movement), *wh*-Movement, and the rules which I claim collapse into the rule "Hop C" (for example, Affix Hopping, Particle Movement, Subject-Aux Inversion, and perhaps Quantifier Floating) were held to be members of the same component. Various proposals have been advanced as to how to group these rules into natural subclasses. Within the metatheory constructed here, I am claiming that all of the relations effected by the rules mentioned above can be collapsed into two maximally general rules: "Move α" and "Hop C." If correctly ordered and filtered by metatheoretical mechanisms, I assert that these rules are sufficient to describe the general domain traditionally held to be the syntactic domain of grammar.

"Hop C": The Core Rule of Inflectional Morphology

We have seen that a fair level of descriptive adequacy can be obtained if a maximally general rule of NP-Movement is allowed to apply freely, provided the outputs of its applications are filtered in the appropriate manner. It will be the task of Chapter 4 to argue that the filters similar to those posited to limit NP-Movement outputs are appropriate for limiting *wh*-Movement applications as well. In this section I address the no less important problem of the formulation of the "local" rules of the grammar. I wish to begin by stating the goal of this section, since it differs in several important respects from the goals of other linguists who have investigated the properties of the "local" rules.

As a point of departure, consider the definition of "Local Transformation" given in Emonds: "Local Transformation: A transformational operation that affects only a sequence of a single nonphrase node C and one adjacent constituent C^1 that is specified without a variable, such that the rule is not subject to any condition *exterior* to C-C^1 (or C^1-C) is called a 'local transformation'" (Emonds, 1976, p. 202). This definition may be thought of as providing, for any transformation, a test for determining whether that transformation belongs to the class of Local Transformations. It is my belief that the definition incorporates an important insight; as I will argue, and as others have argued elsewhere, there are many quite interesting generalizations to be stated concerning transformational applications that are limited to tangent nodes. Focusing on the construct "local movement," however, I do not believe it is necessary to provide a definition of the construct Local Transformation (or Local Movement Transformation). I hold this view since I believe that

what have been analyzed as distinct local movement transformations can be collapsed into one rule—a rule that I will
refer to as "Hop C."

For such a theory of local movement to be maintained,
the task of explication becomes that of defining the operation "hop" on the one hand, and the element "C" on the
other. As in the case of the rule "Move NP," one would expect that a rule formulated with little descriptive machinery,
as Hop C will be, would not in and of itself be sufficient
to partition correctly the class of possible output structures
into the two classes "grammatical" and "ungrammatical."
One would expect, in other words, that such a simple rule
would "overgenerate." Although this expectation is more
than fulfilled, we will see that appeal to filters not specific
to Hop C outputs suffices to narrow in on precisely the desired outputs in a wide range of cases.

On the Movement of the So-Called "Particles"

We may open this inquiry into the properties of local
movement with a consideration of the distribution of particles. The triple given in (115) is a convenient starting point:

(115) (a)   He handed out the papers to the class
     (b)   He handed the papers out to the class
     (c)   *He handed the papers to the class out

Let us accept, without further justification, the analysis of
Emonds (1976), in which particles are analyzed as intransitive prepositions. If we further assume some such phrase
structure rule as (116a) (as opposed to (116b)), we have
(117) as a plausible input to the rule that moves particles.

(116) (a) VP → V NP PP . . .
     (b) VP → V PP NP . . .

(117) He handed $[_{NP}$ the papers$][_{PP}[_P$ out$]]$

$[_{PP}[_P$ to$][_{NP}$ the class$]]$

Let us now state as a condition on the "hop" operation
that it may only relate positions separated by a single con-

stituent. Thus the pairs given in (118) are related by hop, while those in (119) are not, where C, C', C", are constituents, and C' C" is not a constituent.

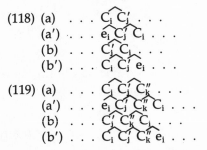

(118) (a)   . . . C_i C_j' . . .
    (a')   . . . e_i C_j' C_i . . .
    (b)   . . . C_j' C_i . . .
    (b')   . . . C_i C_j' e_i . . .

(119) (a)   . . . C_i C_j' C_k'' . . .
    (a')   . . . e_i C_j' C_k'' C_i . . .
    (b)   . . . C_j' C_k'' C_i . . .
    (b')   . . . C_i C_j' C_k'' e_i . . .

As a further condition on the application of hop, we prohibit any derivation that contains more than one application of hop to any element. We preclude, thereby, derivations such as (120) and (121):

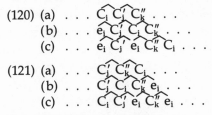

(120) (a)   . . . C_i C_j' C_k'' . . .
    (b)   . . . e_i C_j' C_i C_k'' . . .
    (c)   . . . e_i C_j' e_i C_k'' C_i . . .

(121) (a)   . . . C_j' C_k'' C_i . . .
    (b)   . . . C_j' C_i C_k'' e_i . . .
    (c)   . . . C_i C_j' e_i C_k'' e_i . . .

Concerning the identity of the element that hops, the element "C," let us require that it be nonlexical. Quite simply, I wish to claim that neither members of the categories N, A, V nor their projections may undergo hop. This last stipulation will be refined further below, where it will be argued that such elements as complementizers and determiners are immune to the hopping operation, by virtue of the fact that they have the status of affixes rather than unbound morphemes at the point at which Hop C applies (see Chapter 3).

Given these stipulations, we may consider the application of Hop C to (117).

Consider first the result of applying Hop C to the preposition "to." Note that we have not stipulated the *direction* of movement of Hop C, and that, irrespective of the direction of movement, the output is ungrammatical:

(122) (a) *He handed [$_{NP}$ the papers][$_{P_i}$ to][$_{PP}$[$_P$ out]]

[$_{PP}$[$_{P_i}$ e][$_{NP}$ the class]]

(b) *He handed [$_{NP}$ the papers][$_{PP}$[$_P$ out]][$_{PP}$[$_{P_i}$ e]

[$_{NP}$ the class]][$_{P_i}$ to]

The patterning is not peculiar to the movement of prepositions, however. Note that the movement of verbs must be
similarly conditioned:

(123) (a)   In the hallway [$_{V_i}$ stood][$_{NP}$ a coatrack][$_{VP}$[$_{V_i}$ e]]

(b) *In the hallway [$_{V_i}$ stood][$_{NP}$ John][$_{VP}$[$_{V_i}$ e]

[$_{NP}$ a coatrack]]

It appears that there is a general prohibition, at least in
English, not specific to particles, which precludes movement
of the heads of constituents that contain complements. Thus
the problem of overgeneration occasioned by the possibility
of moving prepositions in transitive prepositional phrases
can be solved quite naturally.

Turning now to the application of Hop C to "out" in (117),
and bearing in mind that we have made no stipulation concerning the direction of movement of that operation, we
note that the problem of ruling out (124) remains.

(124) (a)   He handed [$_{P_i}$ out][$_{NP}$ the papers][$_{PP}$[$_{P_i}$ e]]

[$_{PP}$ to the class]

(b) *He handed [$_{NP}$ the papers][$_{PP}$[$_{P_i}$ e]]

[$_{PP}$ to the class][$_{P_i}$ out]

We note, however, that (124b) illustrates a pattern that will
become familiar—the pattern of the Priority Filter. Re-
ducing (124) to its essentials, we have the string (125):

(125) . . . P_i . . . PP_j . . . P_i . . .

In Chapter 4, a filter of the general form (126) will be developed. This filter, it will be argued, applies at PR.

(126) * . . . A_i . . . A_j . . . A_i . . . , $i \neq j$

The elements A_i and A_j must be "alike" in a sense to be specified; differences in bar-specification (and, as will be seen directly, features assigned by redundancy rules) will not preclude "alikeness" between constituents. I delay the statement of this filter for reasons of exposition.

It appears that although structures in which particles (prepositions) have hopped over prepositional phrases are in general ungrammatical, as the Priority Filter predicts, there are some structures in which particles seem to have hopped over adverbs which are allowed:

(127) He handed the papers $\begin{Bmatrix} \text{slowly} \\ \text{grudgingly} \end{Bmatrix}$ out to the class

The independent capability of adverbs to move makes it difficult to determine whether (127) is an instance of the hopping of "out," however.

We may continue this discussion of particles with the observation that examples such as (128) are precluded by the restriction that an element may not hop over a nonconstituent.

(128) (a) *John out_i handed the papers e_i to the class
    (b) *John handed the papers e_i to the class for Mary out_i

It is worthwhile to note in this context that a structure such as (129) may not undergo Hop C to yield (129b):

(129) (a) $[_{NP_i}$ The papers] were $[_{Adj}$ handed$][_{NP_i}$ e]
$[_{PP}[_P$ out]]

    (b) *$[_{NP_i}$ The papers] were $[_{P_j}$ out$][_{Adj}$ handed$][_{NP_i}$ e]
$[_{PP}[_{P_j}$ e]]

The necessity of blocking (129b) forces a more precise statement of the condition of the operation "hop," namely, that only a single constituent may be hopped over. The point to focus on, and the source of the problem, is that there is an analysis of (129) of the form (130).

(130) . . . P_j Adj P_j . . .

The e of the trace $[_{NP_i} e]$ is the identity element; therefore in (129a) we have the equivalent terminal strings (131a) and (131b):

(131) (a) the, papers, were, handed, e, out
(b) the, papers, were, handed, out

We must, therefore, state the relevant restriction as follows:

(132) *a PM containing a string of the form
. . . C_i vbl e_i . . . ,
(or . . . e_i vbl C_i . . .)
where C_i and e_i are related by Hop C, and $X_1, \ldots, X_n$
= vbl, if $X_1, \ldots, X_n$ is not a constituent

If it is required that (132) inspect all strings of a phrase marker, the desired result with respect to the examples in (129) is obtained.

We can complete this brief discussion of the properties of the movement of prepositions by considering a rather interesting problem raised by sentences such as (133):[17]

(133) (a) The secretary sent the stockholders out a schedule
(b) The professor handed the students out the exam
(c) He has brought Dad down some cigars

As Emonds (1976) has pointed out, the particle may appear only between the two NPs in such constructions; the examples in (134) and (135) are ungrammatical:

(134) (a) *The secretary sent out the stockholders a schedule
(b) *The professor handed out the students the exam
(c) *He has brought down Dad some cigars

(135) (a) *The secretary sent the stockholders a schedule out
(b) *The professor handed the students the exam out
(c) *He has brought Dad some cigars down

We have two different questions to ask: (1) what is the position of the particle at the point of application of Hop C, and (2) why, apparently, can Hop C not apply to such structures?

The first question appears to have a unique solution, given our acceptance of the hypothesis that lexical NPs must be assigned Case. If Oblique is assigned to NPs immediately following V, we must assume a structure as in (136) at the point of Case assignment; (137) and (138) would block assignment of Case to one of the NPs following P.

(136) $[_{VP}[_{V'}$ V NP] NP $[_{PP}$ P]]

(137) (a) $[_{VP}[_{V'}$ V NP][$_{PP}$ P] NP]

    (b) $[_{VP}$ V NP $[_{PP}$ P] NP]

(138) $[_{VP}[_{V'}$ V $[_{PP}$ P] NP] NP]

In (137), the final NP will not be assigned Oblique; in (138) the first NP will not be.

We have just assumed that an NP receives Case only if it is adjacent to V. An alternative suggestion was developed above, however, that V assigns Case to those NPs that it is subcategorized for. If this suggestion is adopted, the structure given in (139) is an available alternative, the choice depending on the form of the particular subcategorization statements involved. We leave this question open here.

(139) $[_{VP}$ V NP NP $[_{PP}$ P]]

Assuming the conclusion that (136) (or (139)) is the SS of (133) to be secure, we note that there is no problem in explaining why the examples in (134) are ungrammatical. Under this analysis, these would constitute examples in which either Hop C applied twice, which is precluded by the definition of the operation "hop," or else Hop C moved an element across a nonconstituent, which is again precluded. The problem, rather, is to determine why the examples of (135) are ungrammatical; the problem is apparently not relevant to the statement of the optional rule Hop C, since the rule has not applied in these examples.

This problem is not peculiar to double-NP constructions; the examples in (140) are also ungrammatical:

(140) (a) *The professor handed the papers to the class out
    (b) *The professor handed the papers yesterday out

Note that the Priority Filter is not itself sufficient to rule out examples such as (140a). Example (140a) *is* excluded if (141) is the only possible source:

(141) The professor handed the papers out to the class

What, however, is to prevent the *surface structure* (142), which would yield (140a) if Hop C did not apply?

(142) The professor handed the papers to the class out

Whatever the answer to this question may be, it can be shown to involve considerations that are not relevant to Hop C, for consider the examples in (143) and (144):

(143) (a) The secretary sent [a schedule] [out from the office] [to the stockholders]
(b) He has brought [some cigars] [down the stairs] [to his father]

(144) (a) *The secretary sent [a schedule] [to the stockholders] [out from the office][18]
(b) *He has brought [some cigars] [to his father] [down the stairs]

The ungrammaticality of the examples in (144), as contrasted with those in (143), demonstrates that there must exist some principle independent of Hop C that orders PP constituents in VP. As would be expected, this principle applies equally to "particle" constructions; I assume that the examples in (135), (140), and (144) are data that fall under this generalization. Whether this generalization should be stated at a level prior to Hop C, such as SS, or after Hop C, I do not know. The metatheory presented here does prevent an analysis in which PPs are moved over other PPs, however, since this would create Priority Filter violations.

On the Hopping of Auxiliary Elements

STRUCTURAL ASSUMPTIONS

I will begin this analysis of the auxiliary elements with the well-founded assumption that the modals and the perfect and progressive aspects belong to the category V, which is analyzed as consisting of the distinctive features $[+V, -N]$. I will furthermore assume that a projection of $[+V, -N]$ is generated between NP and PRED (itself being a projection of [+V, −N]) and that two occurrences of [+V, −N] are generated in PRED before VP (which is a projection of [+V, −N]). A structure such as (145) will be allowed.

(145)

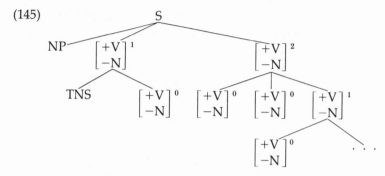

For reasons that will become clear shortly, we will wish to stipulate that the [+V, −N]¹ node that corresponds to the AUX of many current analyses is obligatory (although there are alternatives to TNS, as will be discussed below), whereas the [+V, −N]⁰ nodes that are in AUX or sister to VP are optional.

Considering the verbs "have" and "be," we notice that there are three distinct positions into which they might be inserted: in AUX, in PRED as sister to VP, and in the main verb position.

Suppose we assume that the rules of lexical insertion for "have" and "be" are in fact maximally simple and do not distinguish among the [+V, −N] positions in (145). This quite simple proposal has apparently ideal results, given the data in (146):

(146) (a) Has John left, is John leaving
     (b) John may have left, John may be leaving
     (c) John has a problem, John is a problem

The analysis implicit in (146a) is that inverted auxiliaries are generated in the AUX node; the motivation for this will be discussed directly. In (146b), we have aspects sister to VP, whereas in (146c), we have the main verbs.

Let us now distinguish the main verb from the others by formulating the redundancy rule given in (147):

$$(147) \quad \text{assign } [+\text{AUX}] \: / \: \ldots \: \begin{bmatrix} \overline{} \\ +V \\ -N \end{bmatrix} \begin{bmatrix} +V \\ -N \end{bmatrix} \ldots$$

assign $[-\text{AUX}]$ otherwise

This mechanism, which will be discussed below, allows us to assign to members of the category $[+\text{AUX}, +V, -N]$, but not $[+V, -N]$, the internal lexical structure of a stem in construction with an affix. Among these are the forms "have $\widehat{\text{EN}}$" and "be $\widehat{\text{ING}}$." Specifically, I assume the rule of lexical structure given in (148):

$$(148) \quad \begin{bmatrix} +V \\ -N \\ +\text{AUX} \end{bmatrix}^0 \rightarrow \: {}^[\begin{bmatrix} +V \\ -N \\ +\text{AUX} \end{bmatrix}^0 \: \widehat{\Delta]\,(\text{AFFIX})}$$

We may now be more explicit as regards the variable status of the verbs "have" and "be." Let us distinguish between the perfective "have" and the main verb "have" by stating that the first is subcategorized for EN but not the second. The progressive "be," but not the main verb, will be subcategorized for ING. It now follows, given (148), that the perfect and progressive aspects may only appear in the AUX and sister to VP positions, as desired. Since, however, the main verbs "have" and "be," like other main verbs, do not subcategorize affixes, we have the result that the main verbs may appear in any of the positions in (145) since the presence of the affix in (148) is (crucially) optional. This formulation allows us to posit the lexical insertion rule given in (149), which will insert "have" and "be" into AUX or main verb positions, since the rule does not specify the feature $[\pm\text{AUX}]$.

$$(149) \quad \Delta \rightarrow \begin{Bmatrix} \text{have} \\ \text{be} \end{Bmatrix} \: / \: \ldots \: [\begin{bmatrix} +V \\ -N \end{bmatrix} \: \Delta \: \ldots] \ldots$$

Not all verbs have this freedom, of course. Verbs such as "leave" will only be inserted into $[+V, -N, -\text{AUX}]$ positions.

Continuing to assume that it is the AUX element that inverts in questions (and other constructions), the SS of "has

John money" will be as in (150):

$$(150) \quad [_{NP} \text{ John}] [\begin{bmatrix} +V \\ -N \\ +AUX \end{bmatrix}]^1 \quad \text{TNS} [\begin{bmatrix} +V \\ -N \\ +AUX \end{bmatrix}]^0 \text{ have}]]$$

$$[\begin{bmatrix} +V \\ -N \\ -AUX \end{bmatrix}]^2 [\begin{bmatrix} +V \\ -N \\ -AUX \end{bmatrix}]^1 [\begin{bmatrix} +V \\ -N \\ -AUX \end{bmatrix}]^0 \Delta] [_{NP} \text{ money}]]]$$

The Δ verb in (150) causes no special difficulties as regards selection of the object; we may assume either that "have" controls this position or that it is ignored in the statement of selection from AUX position.[19] I assume a parallel derivation for sentences such as "is John crazy."

Note that we remove the need for a rule of Shift, appealed to in other analyses, by simplifying the rule of lexical insertion for the elements "have" and "be." As regards the application of Hop C, we note that the assignment of the feature [+AUX] allows us to sharpen our definition of C. We may now state that if a nonterminal node H contains the feature αF, and (1) αF is +N or +V, and (2) there is no +G in H, where G is not N or V, then H does not belong to C. This will allow Hop C to apply to [+V, $-$N, +AUX] or [$-$V, $-$N], but not [+V, $-$N, $-$AUX], [$-$V, +N], or [+V, +N]. Following this conception, we may assign the feature complex [+V, $-$N, +AFFIX] to the verbal affixes, a class which includes TNS, EN, ING, and perhaps a few others. The element NOT apparently is not a member of [+V, $-$N, +AFFIX], given its occurrence as the specifier of quantifiers ("not many"), and its occurrence as a free morpheme ("he said not"). We have the option of adding as a necessary condition for membership in C that an element have the feature composition [αV, βN, . . .], and providing a feature complex for SPEC that does not contain [αV, βN]. One consequence of these assumptions will be that NOT does not undergo Hop C; this question is examined in the next section. An alternative account of SPEC as it relates to Hop C is discussed in Chapter 3. Possibilities of execution are numerous here. We will adopt the tentative proposals made here and turn to the application of Hop C to AUX.

AUX HOPPING

We are now in a position to consider the application of Hop C to the structures developed. It is convenient to begin with the process commonly referred to by the term "Subject-Aux Inversion."

Assume what will be motivated below: that TNS and the other affixes undergo Hop C. Given the SS (151), applications of Hop C will yield (152):

(151) John $\left[\begin{bmatrix} +V \\ -N \\ +AUX \end{bmatrix}\right]^1$ PAST $\left[\begin{bmatrix} +V \\ -N \\ +AUX \end{bmatrix}\right]^0$ be $\widehat{ING}$]]

$\left[\begin{bmatrix} +V \\ -N \\ -AUX \end{bmatrix}\right]^2\left[\begin{bmatrix} +V \\ -N \\ -AUX \end{bmatrix}\right]^1\left[\begin{bmatrix} +V \\ -N \\ -AUX \end{bmatrix}\right]^0$ laugh]]]

(152) John $\left[\begin{bmatrix} +V \\ -N \\ +AUX \end{bmatrix}\right]^1$ e$\left[\begin{bmatrix} +V \\ -N \\ +AUX \end{bmatrix}\right]^0$ be PAST]]

$\left[\begin{bmatrix} +V \\ -N \\ -AUX \end{bmatrix}\right]^2\left[\begin{bmatrix} +V \\ -N \\ -AUX \end{bmatrix}\right]^1\left[\begin{bmatrix} +V \\ -N \\ -AUX \end{bmatrix}\right]^0$ laugh $\widehat{ING}$]]]

Consider the possible applications of Hop C to the AUX node $[+V, -N, +AUX]^1$ in (152):

    (153) (a) Was John laughing
         (b) *John laughing was

The problem we face is to explain why (153b) is ungrammatical.

Considering the structure of (153b), given in (154), we notice that the AUX and PRED nodes are not featurally alike:

(154) John $\left[\begin{bmatrix} +V \\ -N \\ +AUX \end{bmatrix}\right]^1$ e]$\left[\begin{bmatrix} +V \\ -N \\ -AUX \end{bmatrix}\right]^2$ · · ·]$\left[\begin{bmatrix} +V \\ -N \\ +AUX \end{bmatrix}\right]^1$ was]

We have already discussed the fact that differences in the bar-specifications of nodes are not relevant to the application of the Priority Filter. Consequently, this difference between the AUX and PRED nodes is not a barrier to the application of the Priority Filter to (154). The distinction between [+AUX] and [−AUX] nodes also is not a barrier once it is realized that in general those features that are assigned by rule, including the features of Case and number, are not relevant to the application of the Priority Filter. In this regard the "alikeness" relation parallels the "nondistinctness" relation of Chomsky.[20] We conclude that, by assuming the Priority Filter, Hop C may be extended to encompass the Subject-Aux Inversion generalization.

We may begin our discussion of the Affix Hopping phenomenon with a consideration of the possibilities afforded by SS (155):

$$(155) \text{ John } \left[\begin{matrix} +V \\ -N \\ +AUX \end{matrix}\right]_1 \text{PAST] leave}$$

The rule Hop C may apply to PAST, yielding either (156a) or (156b):

$$(156) \text{ (a) } \text{ PAST John } \left[\begin{matrix} +V \\ -N \\ +AUX \end{matrix}\right]_1 \text{e] leave}$$

$$\text{(b) John } \left[\begin{matrix} +V \\ -N \\ +AUX \end{matrix}\right]_1 \text{e] leave PAST}$$

The element PAST, which, like PRES, EN, and ING, is a verbal affix, may now be suffixed onto "leave" by the following rule:

$$(157) \ldots S B \ldots \rightarrow \ldots [[S] B] \ldots$$
where S is a stem and B is an affix

I assume that the classes of possible stems and affixes are lexically stipulated; Chapter 3 contains discussion of this point.

I believe that the rule (157) constitutes an important generalization concerning inflectional morphology in English:

that it is suffixation. It would be a mistake, given this generalization, to incorporate a statement of the suffixation process into a particular rule of Affix Hopping, since the behavior of the Case features and the features of number are in all relevant respects parallel to TNS, ING, and EN. If we stipulate that these affixes are intrinsically bound,[21] we may allow (157) to be optional; the rule will apply to (156b) to yield (158):

$$(158) \text{ John } [\begin{bmatrix} +V \\ -N \\ +AUX \end{bmatrix} _1 \text{ e][[leave] PAST]}$$

If, however, (157) does not apply to (156b), the result will be ungrammatical, since it will include a free occurrence of an intrinsically bound morpheme.

The ungrammaticality of (156a), if taken as a member of PR, is also explained, since it contains a free occurrence of PAST.

It is necessary at this point to digress somewhat to consider the distribution of the auxiliary element "do." We know, first, that "do" may not precede the other auxiliary elements; the examples of (159) show this:

(159) (a) *John did could leave
(b) *John did have left
(c) *John did be smiling

When unstressed, "do" may appear either inverted, before a negative, or in constructions involving ellipsis; before the main verb, when this verb is phonologically realized, "do" must be stressed.

(160) (a) Did John leave
(b) John $\begin{cases} \text{did not} \\ \text{didn't} \end{cases}$ leave
(c) Bill didn't leave but John díd

(161) (a) *John díd leave
(b) John díd leave

It appears, consequently, that there is a phonological rule that (obligatorily) stresses "do" if it immediately precedes a phonologically realized main verb; the rest of the distribution may be expressed by the following rule of lexical insertion:

$$(162) \quad e \rightarrow do \; / \; \dots \; \left[\begin{matrix} +V \\ -N \\ +AUX \end{matrix} \right]^1 TNS$$

$$\left[\begin{matrix} +V \\ -N \\ +AUX \end{matrix} \right]^0 \underline{\quad}]\!][\begin{matrix} +V \\ -N \\ -AUX \end{matrix}]^X] \dots$$

Insertion of "do" will be possible only when the optional element $[+V, -N, +AUX]^0$ is generated: when it is, "John did leave" may be derived; when it is not, "John left" may be. The stipulation that the following element be $[-AUX]$ serves to rule out (159a) through (c).

We note that "did John leave" can only be treated as hopping of the AUX node, as the reader can verify.

A refinement of the analysis presented here serves to explain the distribution of the elements *not* and *n't*. Restricting ourselves first to description, we note that *n't* only appears as a suffix of tensed $[+AUX]$ verbs.

(163) (a)   To have not been on time was a pity
(b) *To haven't been on time was a pity

(164) (a)   He may have not been listening
(b) *He may haven't been listening

(165) *He leftn't

The element *not*, on the other hand, only occurs before tenseless verbs.[22]

(166) Not to have been on time was a pity[23]

(167) (a)   He could not do it
(b) *He not could do it

The distribution may be captured in the following way. Let us first assume that *not* may be generated before any verbal stem. This will allow sentences such as (168), which seem syntactically possible if difficult to interpret.

(168) You couldn't not have been not scared

We may assume that each *not* is prefixed to its following verb in this example; structures such as (169) will be generated freely:

$$(169) \quad [_{[+V]} \widehat{not \ V}]$$

It is probably the case that *not* should be analyzed as SPEC of V; if this is done, we will have, more precisely, structures of the form (170):

$$(170) \quad [_{[+V]^1} [_{SPEC} not] [_{[+V]^0} X]]$$

A rule that prefixes specifiers, which will be discussed in more detail in Chapter 3, will yield (171):

$$(171) \quad [_{[+V]^1} [_{[+V]^0} not [_{[+V]^0} X]]]$$

As will be discussed in Chapter 3, the Prefixation rule precedes Hop C; since Hop C cannot analyze elements within words (in this case, a member of the $[+V]^0$ category), prefixes are immune to Hop C.[24]

These observations are relevant to the explanation of the following contrasts:

(172) (a) ?*He could not not do it
     (b) He couldn't not do it

(173) (a) ?*He has not not been working
     (b) He hasn't not been working

Let us consider *not* the prefix form of the morpheme NOT and *n't* its suffix form. If this is correct, (172a) and (173a) will be ungrammatical due to the structural prohibition against any category having more than one specifier. But we have raised a question: What is the source of *n't*?

Given our assumptions, *n't* cannot arise in SPEC. We know, however, that *n't* is dependent on the presence of tense. Consequently, we propose the following phrase structure rules:[25]

$$(174) \ (a) \quad \begin{bmatrix} +V \\ -N \\ +AUX \end{bmatrix}^1 \rightarrow \left\{ \begin{matrix} SPEC \\ \widehat{TNS \ (NOT)} \end{matrix} \right\} \begin{bmatrix} +V \\ -N \\ +AUX \end{bmatrix}^0$$

(b) SPEC → (NOT)

Given these rules, the prefix *not*, if analyzed as SPEC, will be possible only if TNS is not chosen, as desired. An example of the alternative is (175):

(175) John $\left[\begin{matrix} +V \\ -N \\ +AUX \end{matrix}\right]_1$ TNS N͡OT $\left[\begin{matrix} +V \\ -N \\ +AUX \end{matrix}\right]_0$ hav͡e EN]] leave

The most uniform description would be that NOT can never undergo Hop C unless it is in construction with TNS, which does undergo that rule. However, NOT is like TNS, EN, and ING in being an intrinsically bound verbal affix. Consider the application of Hop C to the element TN͡S NOT. The hopping of this element to the left will be ungrammatical, since TNS will be free at PR. TN͡S NOT is not a member of SPEC, and therefore it cannot undergo prefixation. If the unprefixed element TN͡S NOT does not move by Hop C, again the result will be a free occurrence of TNS at PR. We consider next the two possible rightward applications of Hop C.

(176) (a) John $\left[\begin{matrix} +V \\ -N \\ +AUX \end{matrix}\right]_1$ e $\left[\begin{matrix} +V \\ -N \\ +AUX \end{matrix}\right]_0$

have TN͡S NOT EN]] leave

(b) John $\left[\begin{matrix} +V \\ -N \\ +AUX \end{matrix}\right]_1$ e $\left[\begin{matrix} +V \\ -N \\ +AUX \end{matrix}\right]_0$

hav͡e EN TN͡S NOT]] leave

Concerning (176a), notice that if EN does not hop rightward, it can only undergo Suffixation if it is to be bound at PR. But if EN is suffixed to "have," "have" will have two members of the same class of affixes, EN and TNS, as affixes. Precluding this by a general principle, which principle also suffices to entail the impossibility of two specifiers on a stem, two Cases on a noun, two numbers on a noun, and so forth, we have as the only well-formed continuation of (176a) the hopping of EN, which, as the reader can verify, may only be to the right, as desired. Applications of Suf-

fixation will yield "John hasn't left." The general theory put
forward allows only this derivation; as the reader can verify,
any other applications of Hop C yield structures ruled out
at PR. Concerning (176b), we notice that no further application of Hop C can salvage it; if it remains unchanged, the
principle precluding two affixes of the same class on a single
stem rules it out at PR.

We have now explained why *"John not has left" is ungrammatical. Since "not" is a prefix, and two occurrences of
the same affix are precluded, we have also distinguished
between "John hasn't not left" and ?*"John has not not left."
As for *"John may haven't left," we notice that the only possible source is (177):

$$(177) \text{ John } \left[\begin{matrix} +V \\ -N \\ +AUX \end{matrix}\right]^1 \text{ TNS} \overgroup{\text{ NOT}} \left[\begin{matrix} +V \\ -N \\ +AUX \end{matrix}\right]$$

may]][[have $\overgroup{\text{EN}}$] leave]

But here we run into a problem. TNS $\overgroup{\text{NOT}}$ may hop over
"may," "have" over "not," and EN over "leave" to yield
*"John may haven't left," after Suffixation. There is a related
difficulty with regard to "John may have left." Consider its
source:

$$(178) \text{ John TNS may have } \overgroup{\text{EN}} \text{ leave}$$

What prevents *"John may haven leave," if TNS hops over
"may" but EN does not hop?

Both problems may be solved by the stipulation that
modals are generated with affixes, making them parallel to
"have $\overgroup{\text{EN}}$" and "be $\overgroup{\text{ING}}$." The affix of a modal is $\emptyset$, and will
belong to the same class as TNS, ING, and EN. Given this,
the source of "John may have left" will be not (178), but
(179):

$$(179) \text{ John TNS may } \overgroup{\emptyset \text{ have}} \overgroup{\text{ EN}} \text{ leave}$$

For now familiar reasons, TNS can only hop to the right, but
this forces the other affixes to do likewise if the Two Affix
Prohibition is to be avoided.

Returning now to *"John may haven't left," we have not (177) but (180) as the source:

(180) John TNS⌢NOT may⌢∅ have⌢EN leave

If TNS NOT hops "may," we will have (181):

(181) John e may TNS⌢NOT ∅ have⌢EN leave

Only if NOT hops ∅ and "have" hops NOT will we have (182), which, after ∅ hops "have," EN hops "leave," and Suffixation, will yield *"John may haven't left."

(182) John e may TNS e ∅ have NOT e EN leave

But necessary to this derivation was an application of Hop C to NOT, precluded unless it hops with TNS. Since by the definition of "Hop" no element may hop twice, we have the desired result.

Notice that if TNS⌢NOT hops "may⌢∅" to produce (183a), and TNS hops NOT, "have" hops TNS, and EN hops "leave," we will have (183b):

(183) (a) John e may⌢∅ TNS⌢NOT have⌢EN leave
      (b) John e may ∅ e NOT have TNS e e leave EN
            (*John mayn't had left)[26]

In this derivation, which avoids the Two Affix Prohibition, TNS hops twice, first in construction with NOT and then alone. But since NOT cannot hop alone, TNS and TNS⌢NOT are presumably nondistinct as regards the application of Hop C.[27] Consequently, (183b) violates the prohibition against any element hopping twice.

But there is another, more apparent, violation in the derivation of (183b). Consider the application of Hop C to "have," which, more explicitly, will produce (184b) given (184a):

(184) (a) . . . NOT $\left[\begin{matrix} +V \\ -N \\ +AUX \end{matrix}\right]^0 \left[\begin{matrix} +V \\ -N \\ +AUX \end{matrix}\right]^0$ have]

$\left[\begin{matrix} +V \\ -N \\ +AFFIX \end{matrix}\right]^0$ EN]] . . .

(b) . . . $\left[\begin{bmatrix} +V \\ -N \\ +AUX \end{bmatrix}^0 \text{have}\right]$ NOT $\left[\begin{bmatrix} +V \\ -N \\ +AUX \end{bmatrix}^0\right]$

$\left[\begin{bmatrix} +V \\ -N \\ +AUX \end{bmatrix}^0 e\right]\left[\begin{bmatrix} +V \\ -N \\ +AFFIX \end{bmatrix}^0 \text{EN}\right]$ . . .

This application violates the general prohibition mentioned above against the movement of the heads of constituents. I assume that the head of a constituent may differ featurally from it only with respect to bar-specification; in the structure considered here, the head of the containing node does not differ from it even in this regard. Furthermore, if EN hops to the right *before* "have" hops to the left, we will have the structure (185):

(185) . . . $\left[\begin{bmatrix} +V \\ -N \\ +AUX \end{bmatrix}^0\begin{bmatrix} +V \\ -N \\ +AUX \end{bmatrix}^0 \text{have}\right]$

$\left[\begin{bmatrix} +V \\ -N \\ +AFFIX \end{bmatrix}^0 e\right]$ V $\left[\begin{bmatrix} +V \\ -N \\ +AFFIX \end{bmatrix}^0 \text{EN}\right]$

But if "have" hops to the left, the violation against the movement of heads again applies, since it would be a complication of this principle to formalize it so as to distinguish between constituents and their traces (in this case, the trace of EN).

Considering the matter somewhat more abstractly, we note that by generating structures such as (186) with the PS rules and appealing to a general principle prohibiting the movement of heads, we entail a quite specific result: we entail the classical rule of Affix Hopping.

(186) $\left[\begin{bmatrix} +V \\ -N \\ +AUX \end{bmatrix}^0\begin{bmatrix} +V \\ -N \\ +AUX \end{bmatrix}^0 X\right]\left[\begin{bmatrix} +V \\ -N \\ +AFFIX \end{bmatrix}^0 Y\right]$

Recall that we have entailed that the affix may not move to the left. We have also entailed that the auxiliary verb X may not move alone in either direction. Furthermore, the entire representation in (186) may not hop over any member of the category [+V, −N], which includes both main verbs and auxiliaries, due to the Priority Filter. Due to the stipulation that the affixes are intrinsically bound, the Two Affix Prohibition, and the PS rule positioning TNS before the auxiliaries, we have entailed that the affixes must move to the right.

Return for a moment to consider (185) and assume that V is [+V, −N, +AUX]. Why, it should be asked, does the application of Hop C not violate the Priority Filter? The answer is that the [+AFFIX] feature is not assigned by a redundancy rule, as [−AUX] is, and thus the verb and affix are featurally distinct. Furthermore, as will be discussed in Chapter 4, it is necessary to formulate the Priority Filter in such a way that each element in it c-commands the following one. The application in (185), consequently, does not meet the structural description of the Priority Filter, as desired.

We may now attend to the fact that there is a certain redundancy in the prohibition against moving heads and our definition of C. Suppose we formulated Hop C as follows:

(187) Hop C only if C is not a head

What else must be stated? The hopping of PP (Particle Movement) is not affected, nor is the hopping of AUX. We have seen that the correct result as regards the hopping of affixes is independently assured. What if we dropped the featural definition of C given above and allowed Hop C to apply to NP, AP, and VP? The hopping of NP would appear to cause difficulties if the source of particles in double-NP constructions is as in (188):

(188) V NP NP PP

Hopping could yield first (189a) and then (189b):

(189) (a) V NP PP NP e
      (b) V e PP NP NP e

We would derive *"they sent out the stockholders the letters," which is blocked if NP does not belong to C. The hopping of AP and VP also appears to raise difficulties. Consequently, we retain the restriction that C may belong to N, A, or V or their projections only if it is marked in some way (in the cases considered, by [+AFFIX] or [+AUX]). Perhaps, with sufficient care, a means of dropping even this restriction could be found, but I will not pursue this possibility further here.

Returning now to the analysis of the auxiliary system, there are a few loose ends concerning the distribution of *not* and *n't* that deserve to be tied up. Consider the contrast in (190):

> (190) (a)   I decided to not do it[28]
> (b)   *I decided ton't do it

(190b) is ruled out due to the incompatibility of "to" and TNS. In "I decided not to do it," "not" is prefixed to "to," and in (190a) "not" is prefixed to "do." The contrast between (191a) and (191b) is explained once it is stated as a general principle that a phonologically unrealized stem may never have a phonologically realized affix (the prefix "not," in this case):[29]

> (191) (a)   I decided not to
> (b)   *I decided to not

Other tenseless constructions, for example the "subjunctive" and the gerund, pattern as predicted:[30]

> (192) (a)   I demand that he not have left before I return
> (b)   I demand that he have not left before I return
> (c)   *I demand that he haven't left before I return

> (193) (a)   I resent his not having returned
> (b)   I resent his having not returned
> (c)   *I resent his havingn't returned

In the (a) and (b) examples, *not* is SPEC; since non-SPEC NOT, the source of *n't*, only occurs with TNS, the (c) examples are precluded.

A remaining problem is to preclude *"he leftn't." Its source would be (194):

(194) he $[_{\begin{bmatrix} +V \\ -N \\ +AUX \end{bmatrix}}{}^1$ TNŜ NOT] leave

Apparently we must stipulate that NOT subcategorizes a member of the $[+V, -N, +AUX]^0$ category; (194) will now violate a subcategorization statement, but (195) will be well formed, where Δ may be filled by any auxiliary, including "do."

(195) he $[_{\begin{bmatrix} +V \\ -N \\ +AUX \end{bmatrix}}{}^1$ TNŜ NOT $[_{\begin{bmatrix} +V \\ -N \\ +AUX \end{bmatrix}}{}^0 \Delta]]$ leave

The reader who has followed the argumentation to this point may well have noted alternative means of executing the general ideas presented, and perhaps even errors in the execution itself. Given the minimal nature of the descriptive apparatus appealed to, the number of derivations to be inspected is quite large, and possibilities for oversight are great. Furthermore, the auxiliary system exhibits many complex regularities, and the choice as to which of these are central is a difficult one. I believe, however, that the utility of Hop C in the description of this baroque construction has been established.

A FINAL NOTE ON THE HOPPING OF QUANTIFIERS

Although pairs such as (196) and (197) would appear to be easily handled by Hop C, the contrast in (198) gives us pause.

(196) (a) All the men left
     (b) The men all left

(197) (a) The men all have left
     (b) The men have all left

(198) (a) All the men haven't left
     (b) The men all haven't left
     (c) The men haven't all left

In (198c), the sole interpretation places "all" within the scope of *n't*, whereas (198a) and (198b), depending on intonation, are ambiguous in this regard. Consequently, it would appear that all of (198a) through (c) should belong to SS. There are strict conditions on the movement of quantifiers, as discussed in Fiengo and Lasnik (1976); these might be stated as filters at SS (or PR) if "Move Quantifier," not Hop C, is the appropriate rule. The choice between these two possibilities depends to a great extent, I believe, on what the appropriate treatment of the scope of negation is in REST. It is clear that the assignment of the scope of negation is sensitive to stress; on the other hand, structural relations expressed at the level of SS (such as "not many people," and so forth) also play a role. In the absence of a theory that decides at what level sentences such as (198c) are to receive interpretation, I leave the question open as to whether Hop C subsumes the movement of quantifiers.[31]

In this chapter, the general question has been raised as to what the class of structures is that determines LF (and SR). It has been found possible to factor out a class of syntactic dependencies which can be subsumed under Hop C and which appear to make no contribution to LF (or SR). I believe it appropriate to dub the component whose core rule is Hop C the component of Inflectional Morphology. On the other hand, a very general movement rule affecting NPs and *wh*-elements has been found to create structures that do determine LF (and SR). Much of the descriptive burden in this approach has been borne by filters applying at the various levels. While there are many alternative executions of analysis possible, given the idea that there are autonomous "hop" and "move" components, I believe this idealization to be near to optimal, and I will assume it in the next chapter, which deals with the behavior of complementizers.

3
Complementizer Allomorphy

It was a primary consideration in the latter half of Chapter 2 to define the properties of the operation "Hop C." The element "C" was held to range over the grammatical formatives, into which class I placed all constituents that do not belong to the categories N, A, V, or their projections. This proposal, that all grammatical formatives may hop, appears, at first glance, to be too general; neither determiners nor complementizers appear to undergo any movement operations whatsoever. In this chapter I argue the thesis that the definition of C proposed in Chapter 2 is, in fact, correct, and that the fact that determiners and complementizers cannot hop is only apparently exceptional. The essence of the argument is that both determiners and complementizers undergo an operation that makes them dependents on the elements that follow them. This operation, which I term Prefixation, precedes the rule Hop C. It follows from this that Hop C will not be able to move determiners and complementizers, just as it cannot move other prefixes. Therefore C can be defined as ranging over the grammatical formatives—the apparent counterexamples being eliminated in a principled way.

There is another proposal in this chapter which is as important as the proper definition of C to the construction of the variant of REST presented in this book. Consider the derivational structure that will be developed:

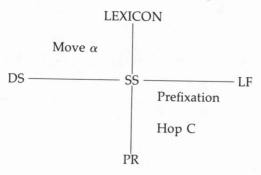

Various aspects of "Move α" have been discussed in Chapter 2. Here it will be argued that if the output of an independently motivated Prefixation rule, which relates SS to PR, is made subject to a filtering mechanism which is itself a principle of morphology constraining word structure, then a quite general account of some quite complex phenomena involving complementizer distribution can be attained. The analysis presented here is not the only analysis of the general class of phenomena extant, nor even the only analysis within the general framework of REST.[1] It does have, however, some quite controversial implications, in particular with regard to the Subjacency Condition. The analysis of complementizers presented here proceeds under the assumption that there are no deletion rules in the grammar; in this respect, the analysis contrasts with that of Chomsky and Lasnik (1977). The relative infinitival construction provides a starting point.

On the Morphology of Complementizers

On the Syntactic Behavior of Infinitival Relatives

While relative clauses in English are, generally speaking, indicative, there are certain environments in which the infinitive is chosen. Typical examples are the following:

(1) (a) She was looking for a pen with which to write
   (b) He found a linguist with whom to correspond
   (c) They built a harpsichord on which to play Bach

There is also a related construction which, to some speakers, sounds less stilted than the sentences in (1). Some examples of this construction are given in (2), and as the examples in (3) indicate, the embedded infinitives are adjuncts to the NPs.[2]

(2) (a) She was looking for a pen to write with
   (b) A linguist to correspond with is a necessity
   (c) They found a harpsichord to play Bach on

(3) (a) *She was looking for it to play Bach on

   (b) *$\begin{Bmatrix} \text{John} \\ \text{He} \end{Bmatrix}$ to correspond with is a necessity

   (c) *They found it to play Bach on

The construction exemplified in (2a) and (2c) can easily be confused with the reduced adverbial purpose clause, given in (4) and (5).

(4) (a) She was looking for a pen (in order) to write with it
   (b) He found a linguist (in order) to correspond with her
   (c) They built a harpsichord (in order) to play Bach on it

(5) (a) She was looking for it (in order) to write with it

   (b) He found $\begin{Bmatrix} \text{John} \\ \text{him} \end{Bmatrix}$ (in order) to correspond with him

   (c) They built it (in order) to play Bach on it

In the reduced purpose clause there is not the "missing constituent" characteristic of the relative, and pronouns and proper names are allowed, as would be expected.

There are some quite peculiar, and largely unstudied, conditions on the selection of the matrix verb in sentences that contain relative infinitivals. Contrast the interpretations of the following pairs, for example:

(6) (a) He was looking for a pen to write with
   (b) He was burning a pen to write with

(7) (a) He built a house in which to live
   (b) He destroyed a house in which to live

(8) (a) He found a friend to play with
   (b) He lost a friend to play with

In each case, the relative clause is "purposive," but in the (b) examples the "purpose" (or use) identified is that of the NP which is the head of the relative clause,[3] while the (a) examples have not only this reading, but one in which the purpose identified is that of the activity specified in the matrix. Interestingly, the definite article seems to force the former interpretation:[4]

(9) (a) He was looking for the pen to write with
   (b) He built the house to live in
   (c) He found the piano to play on

It is not my purpose here to examine these subtleties in detail, however. Rather, I intend to analyze the syntactic behavior of the relative infinitival, and from this analysis to draw some implications for the analysis of complementizers.

There are also examples of the relative infinitival in which the subject of the infinitive is relativized. Their distribution is limited in certain ways that are not clearly understood; if the head is indefinite, it seems that the grammaticality of this construction in subject position is sometimes marginal:[5]

(10) (a) ?A man to do the job walked in
   (b) The man to do the job walked in

(11) (a) Someone to replace Smith should be hired
   (b) The person to replace Smith should have a background in Aztec morphology

(12) (a) We found a man to do the job
   (b) We found the man to do the job

The impossibility of examples such as those in (13) is entailed by the claim that these are, indeed, relative clause structures:

(13) (a) *John to do the job walked in
   (b) *He to replace Smith should have a background in Aztec morphology

ON THE DEPENDENCIES BETWEEN COMPLEMENTIZER
AND SUBJECT POSITIONS

Returning to examples such as those in (1), one notes a curious fact: there are no grammatical examples of the form of (14):

(14) (a) *She was looking for a pen which to write with
    (b) *He found a linguist whom to correspond with
    (c) *They built a harpsichord which to play Bach on

One might expect examples such as those in (14) to be grammatical, since in general the fronting of prepositions is optional in relative clauses:

(15) (a) He found a linguist with whom he could correspond
    (b) He found a linguist whom he could correspond with

It would miss the point to formulate the grammar in such a way that the fronting of the preposition was obligatory in relative infinitivals, however, since examples such as (16) are also impossible:

(16) (a) *He found an instrument which to play
    (b) *She found a topic which to study
    (c) *They constructed a theory which to test

The generalization appears to be that a *wh*-word may appear in a relative infinitival only in case it is preceded by a preposition. One might propose that examples such as (16) are ungrammatical because the relative pronoun obligatorily deletes in relative infinitivals when not preceded by a preposition. This mechanism would have to be independently motivated, however, since the apparent "deletion" of relative pronouns is tensed relative clauses is optional, where possible:

(17) (a) She had a theory (which) she could test

    (b) She had a theory $\begin{Bmatrix} \text{which} \\ *\emptyset \end{Bmatrix}$ proved her correct

The relative infinitival appears even more complex when the influence of lexically filled subjects is considered. Note first that both (18) and (19) are impossible:

(18) (a) *She was looking for a pen with which John to write
(b) *He found a linguist with whom Fran to correspond
(c) *They built a harpsichord on which Wanda to play

(19) (a) *She was looking for a pen which John to write with
(b) *He found a linguist whom Fran to correspond with
(c) *They built a harpsichord which Wanda to play on

But note that the sentences in (20) are grammatical, where "for" is in the position of the relative pronouns.

(20) (a) She was looking for a pen for John to write with
(b) He found a linguist for Fran to correspond with
(c) They built a harpsichord for Wanda to play on

As in the examples in (2), the behavior of pronouns and proper names indicates that the embedded infinitives are adjuncts to the NPs.

(21) (a) *She was looking for it for John to write with

(b) $*\begin{Bmatrix} \text{Jane} \\ \text{She} \end{Bmatrix}$ for John to correspond with is a necessity

(c) *They found it for Wanda to play on

Note further that the entire NPs with their adjuncts can appear in subject position; this environment precludes an analysis in which the complements are analyzed as reduced adverbial purpose clauses:

(22) (a) A pen (*in order) (for John) to write with was sitting on the table
(b) A linguist (*in order) (for John) to correspond with could not be found
(c) A harpsichord (*in order) (for Wanda) to play on was one of her requirements

THE METATHEORETICAL IMPLICATIONS
OF A *wh*-MOVEMENT ANALYSIS

The Specified Subject Condition (Opacity) Given certain assumptions, a plausibility argument can be constructed to show that the construction exemplified in (20) is in fact a relative clause construction, since the only other plausible analyses can be refuted. In principle, one might argue that an example such as (23a) is derived from (23b) by a rule of deletion, or from (23c) by movement.

(23) (a) She found a pen for John to write with
     (b) She found a pen for John to write with a pen
     (c) She found Δ for John to write with a pen

Under this analysis, the rule of Object Deletion operating on (23b), or, conceivably, some formulation of Tough-Movement operating on (23c), would yield (23a),[6] whose derivation would be roughly parallel to that of sentences such as those in (24):

(24) (a) John is too stupid for us to talk to
     (b) Latin is easy for us to learn

There are, however, structural differences between the sentences in (24) and ones such as (23a) which mitigate against this analysis. Note first that the "for" NP strings in (24) appear to be prepositional phrases, not the subjects of embedded Ss. Support for this hypothesis follows from the fact that they can appear after the infinitival complements:

(25) (a) John is too stupid to talk to, for us
     (b) Latin is easy to learn, for us

Now there is evidence that is parallel to that in (25) that "for John" in (23a) can be analyzed as a prepositional phrase:

(26) She found a pen to write with, for John

(23a) appears to be structurally ambiguous, however. When another "for"-prepositional phrase is added, the second "for" NP can only be analyzed as the complementizer and subject of an embedded sentence, as the following examples show:

(27) (a) She found for Fred a pen for John to write with
     (b) She found a pen for John to write with, for Fred
     (c) *She found for Fred a pen to write with, for John

But now consider the fact that (27a) and (27b) are grammatical. If an Object Deletion (or Tough-Movement) analysis were adopted, the rule would apparently have to relate the underlined positions in the following structures:

(28) (a) She found for Fred a pen for John to write with a pen
     (b) She found for Fred $\underline{\Delta}$ for John to write with a pen

However, the Specified Subject Condition (or Opacity) precludes derivations of this type. Examples (27a) contrasts with (29) in this regard:

(29) (a) *John is too stupid for us for them to talk to
     (b) *Latin is easy for us for them to learn

It seems plausible, then, to maintain that (27a) and (27b) are parallel to (30a) and (30b), not to Object Deletion or Tough-Movement constructions:

(30) (a) She found for Fred a pen which John could write with
     (b) She found a pen which John could write with for Fred

There is further evidence motivating a structure such as (31):

(31) She found [$_{NP}$ a pen [$_{\overline{S}}$ for John to write with]]

Note first that a complement such as that in (32) can only be assigned a sentential structure, under standard assumptions:

(32) I couldn't find any topic [$_{\overline{S}}$ for there to be disagreement about]

Second, consider examples such as those in (33):[7]

(33) (a) I can't find anyone (for you) to be employed by
     (b) I can't find anyone by whom to be employed

The stilted character of (33b) apparently derives from considerations not peculiar to relative infinitivals; (34) is similarly stilted:

(34) I can't find anyone by whom you can be employed

In summary, if the Specified Subject Condition (or Opacity) is assumed to be valid, a *wh*-Movement analysis of examples such as (35) seems to be required.

(35) She found for Fred a pen for John to write with

There are, however, several problems with this analysis. As noted above, the ungrammaticality of structures such as those in (36) must be accounted for, among other things.

(36) (a) *She found for Fred a pen which (John) to write with
    (b) *She found for Fred a pen with which John to write

An Objection Raised and Answered Before constructing an explanation of the preceding data using a *wh*-Movement analysis, I wish to answer an objection that might be made to such an attempt. The objection I have in mind proceeds from the observation that examples such as (37) are ungrammatical:

(37) *I am looking for a politician to argue that people should not steal from

The objection continues with the point that if a *wh*-Movement analysis of (37) is assumed, it should be predicted that, all things being equal, (37) should be grammatical, since it is parallel to (38) under such an analysis.

(38) I am looking for a politician whom one could argue that people should not steal from

The criticism might then conclude with the point that, given the fact that (37) is not grammatical, and assuming the successive cyclic application of *wh*-Movement, an Object Deletion or Tough-Movement analysis is called for, since under either analysis the ungrammaticality of (37) would follow from general conditions (for example, Opacity), whereas under a *wh*-Movement analysis, the ungrammaticality is unexplained.

The criticism can be answered directly by pointing out that in fact all things are *not* equal with regard to the behavior of infinitival and tensed relatives. The following contrast provides convincing evidence of this:

(39) (a) *I am looking for a politician from whom to argue that people should not steal
    (b) I am looking for a politician from whom one could argue that people should not steal

The example (39a) can only be derived by *wh*-Movement, assuming the appropriate deep structure, yet (39a) is ungrammatical. I submit that the ungrammaticality of (39a) and the ungrammaticality of (37) may well derive from the same (as yet unspecified) source.[8] But in any event, the fact that (39a) is not grammatical demonstrates that the ungrammaticality of (37) is not in itself evidence against a *wh*-Movement analysis, as the criticism above assumed. I wish to leave open the question of why (37) and (39a) are ungrammatical, and to turn to the construction of an analysis of relative infinitivals utilizing *wh*-Movement, which explains the rather bizarre collection of facts presented above.

An Analysis of Relative Infinitivals

ON THE STRUCTURE OF COMPLEMENTIZERS—
SOME ASSUMPTIONS

Since the work of Bresnan (1972), it has been quite generally assumed that the complementizers are present at the level of deep structure, introduced under the node COMP, which itself is introduced by the phrase structure rule (40):

$$(40) \ \bar{S} \rightarrow COMP \ S$$

I wish, however, to pursue a somewhat different syntactic analysis, introduced in Chapter 2, in which complementizers are members of the category SPEC (of S). Thus there will exist PS-applications of the form (41a), which is an instance of the schema in (41b):

$$(41) \ (a) \ \bar{S} \rightarrow SPEC \ S$$
$$(b) \ X^n \rightarrow SPEC \ X^{n-1}$$

I will assume that SPEC may be [+THAT], which will correspond to THAT, or [−THAT], which will correspond to FOR.

Second, I adopt a metatheory in which all lexical insertion, including that of complementizers, applies at the level of surface structure. In the derivations considered below, I will, for ease of exposition, treat only the SS-insertion of a few of the lexical items under consideration; the others will be represented as though they had been inserted previously.

Third, I assume that the PS-rule expanding SPEC is (42):[9]

$$(42)\ \text{SPEC} \to e$$

The symbol *e* may be replaced by either lexical insertion or *wh*-Movement. I assume that there are no structures in the syntax of modern English, be they surface structures or intermediate structures, of the form (43), where *A* and *B* are not a constituent and belong to the terminal or nonterminal vocabulary.

$$(43)\ \ldots\ [_{\text{SPEC}}[A][B]]\ \ldots$$

This contrasts with the analysis of Chomsky and Lasnik (1977), who, working in a different framework, posit intermediate structures such as those in (44):[10]

(44) (a) $[_{\text{COMP}}[who][that]]$

  (b) $[_{\text{COMP}}[to\ whom][for]]$

  (c) $[_{\text{COMP}}[pictures\ of\ whom][that]]$

Fourth, I will be assuming that there is no rule deleting elements in COMP in the grammar of English.[11] This also contrasts with the proposals of Chomsky and Lasnik (1977), in which a maximally simple rule of this sort is formulated.

Fifth, I will be assuming the existence of a Prefixation rule, which applies between SS and PR.

THE DERIVATION OF RELATIVE INFINITIVALS

Consider the deep structure of an NP such as "a pen for John to write with," which, if it is assumed (1) that the derivation involves *wh*-Movement, and (2) that lexical items (in particular, "for") are inserted at SS, would look roughly as follows:[12]

$$(45)\ [_{\text{NP}}[_{\text{NP}} \cdots]_{\bar{\text{S}}}[_{\text{SPEC}} \begin{bmatrix} -\text{THAT} \\ -\text{WH} \end{bmatrix} \quad e]_{\text{S}} \cdots [_{\text{NP}} \begin{matrix} e \\ [wh] \end{matrix}]]]]$$

wh-Movement will yield (46a), and lexical insertion, (46b):

(46) (a) $[_{NP}[_{NP} \cdots]_{\bar{S}}[_{SPEC} \quad [_{NP} \text{ e}]][_S \cdots [_{NP} \text{ e}]]]]$
$\qquad\qquad \begin{bmatrix} -\text{THAT} \\ -\text{WH} \end{bmatrix} \text{[wh]} \qquad\qquad \text{[wh]}$

(b) $[_{NP}[_{NP} \text{ a pen}]_{\bar{S}}[_{SPEC} \quad [_{NP} \text{ e}]][_S \text{ John to}$
$\qquad\qquad\quad \begin{bmatrix} -\text{THAT} \\ -\text{WH} \end{bmatrix} \text{[wh]}$

write with $[_{NP} \text{ e}]]]]$
$\qquad\qquad \text{[wh]}$

More precisely, all lexical insertion has applied in (46b) with the exception of insertion in the position of SPEC.

Now if *wh*-Insertion and *for*-Insertion apply *in that order*, first (47) and finally (48) will be derived.[13]

(47) $[_{NP}[_{NP} \text{ a pen}]_{\bar{S}}[_{SPEC} \quad [_{NP} \text{ which}]][_S \text{ John to write}$
$\qquad\qquad\qquad \begin{bmatrix} -\text{THAT} \\ -\text{WH} \end{bmatrix} \text{[wh]}$

with $[_{NP} \text{ e}]]]]$
$\qquad \text{[wh]}$

(48) $[_{NP}[_{NP} \text{ a pen}]_{\bar{S}}[_{SPEC} \quad \text{for}][_S \text{ John to write}$
$\qquad\qquad\qquad \begin{bmatrix} -\text{THAT} \\ -\text{WH} \end{bmatrix}$

with $[_{NP} \text{ e}]]]]$
$\qquad \text{[wh]}$

Leaving aside momentarily the problem of the relative order of the two insertion applications, it should be noted that the deletion of $[_{NP}$ which] will be constrained by the
$\qquad\qquad\qquad\qquad\quad \text{[wh]}$
principle of recoverability. In this derivation, the non-distinctness of these features with those of the NP "a pen" will constitute a sufficient condition for a permissible deletion. It should also be pointed out that from the fact that a particular metatheory allows the formulation of a rule whose *effect* is to delete certain elements (under certain conditions), it does not follow that that metatheory must countenance the formulation of a rule such as that given in (49):

(49) Delete α / X____Y

One could, on formal grounds, exclude rules such as (49), which are *formulated as* deletion rules, while allowing, to return to the case at hand, the formulation of an insertion rule, which would, in some derivations, have the *effect* of deletion. It is this option that is taken here.

It should also be mentioned that I am assuming that lexical insertion replaces the entire contents of a nonterminal with a terminal element. While the contents will often be *e* at the point of lexical insertion, examples such as the application that yields (48) will be allowed.

The derivation of an NP such as "a pen to write with" raises difficulties for the analysis as formulated so far. Given deep structure (50), *wh*-Movement will produce (51a), and lexical insertion, (51b):

(50) $[_{NP}[_{NP} \cdots][_{\bar{S}}[_{SPEC} \begin{bmatrix} -THAT \\ -WH \end{bmatrix} \quad e][_{S}[_{NP} \; e] \cdots [_{NP} \; e]_{[wh]}]]]]$

(51) (a) $[_{NP}[_{NP} \cdots][_{\bar{S}}[_{SPEC} \begin{bmatrix} -THAT \\ -WH \end{bmatrix} \; [_{NP} \; e]_{[wh]}]$

$[_{S}[_{NP} \; e] \cdots [_{NP} \; e]_{[wh]}]]]]$

(b) $[_{NP}[_{NP} \; a \; pen][_{\bar{S}}[_{SPEC} \begin{bmatrix} -THAT \\ -WH \end{bmatrix} \; [_{NP} \; e]_{[wh]}]$

$[_{S}[_{NP} \; e] \; to \; write \; with \; [_{NP} \; e]_{[wh]}]]]]$

But now, if *wh*-Insertion and *for*-Insertion apply, as in the previous derivation, (52) will incorrectly be generated:

(52) *a pen for to write with

In response to this problem, I wish to advance two hypotheses. Both of these, when sharpened, would seem plausible candidates for metatheoretical status, and therefore would not need to be stipulated in the grammar.

The first proposal I wish to advance involves the status of complementizers as members of the category SPEC.

As noted in Chomsky and Halle (1968),[14] the surface structure of a string as motivated by syntactic considerations will not, in all cases, be identical to the structure required as input to the phonological component. A classic example of this discrepancy involves phrases such as (53), in which hyphens indicate phonological phrase boundaries, and brackets indicate the motivated syntactic structure.

(53) this is [the cat - that caught [the rat - that stole the cheese]]

Consequently, there must exist a set of readjustment rules whose effect will be to rebracket certain strings into phonological phrases. As an instance of such a rule, I wish to propose (54):

$$(54)\ [_{\alpha^n}[_{SPEC}\ \gamma][_{\alpha^{n-1}}[_\beta\ \cdots\ ]\ \cdots\ ]] \rightarrow$$

$$[_{\alpha^n}[_{\alpha^{n-1}}[_\beta\ [_{SPEC}\ \gamma][_\beta\ \cdots\ ]]\ \cdots\ ]]$$

where γ is a grammatical formative

Given structures such as (55), (54) will apply to yield (56):

$$(55)\ [_{\overline{\overline{N}}}[_{SPEC}\ \gamma][_{\overline{N}}[_N\ \cdots\ ]\ \cdots\ ]]$$

$$(56)\ [_{\overline{\overline{N}}}[_{\overline{N}}[_N\ [_{SPEC}\ \gamma][_N\ \cdots\ ]]\ \cdots\ ]]$$

Similarly, (54) will relate (57) and (58):

$$(57)\ [_{\overline{\overline{S}}}[_{SPEC}\ \gamma][_S\ [_{\overline{\overline{N}}}\ \cdots\ ]\ \cdots\ ]]$$

$$(58)\ [_{\overline{\overline{S}}}[_S\ [_{\overline{\overline{N}}}[_{SPEC}\ \gamma][_{\overline{\overline{N}}}\ \cdots\ ]]\ \cdots\ ]]$$

I will refer to the hypothesis that (54) applies to complementizers (and determiners, and so on) as the Prefixation Hypothesis (PH). The application illustrated in (57) and (58) will account for, among other things, the fact that the phonological breaks in a sentence such as (59) are as indicated.

(59) We believe - that the man - was dishonest
(Cf.: *We believe - that - the man was dishonest)

The hypothesis that complementizers prefix to the following NP has relevance for the analysis of relative infinitivals when this hypothesis is conjoined with another principle, which involves morphological structure:

(60) *. . . $[_\alpha \gamma [_\beta \delta]]$ . . . (or . . . $[_\alpha [_\beta \delta] \gamma]$ . . .)

where (i) γ is affixed to δ
and (ii) δ is phonologically null and γ is phonologically realized

While the Prefixation Rule applies between SS and the component of inflectional morphology, I assume that (60) applies at PR. The rationale for this will become apparent directly. I will refer to the filter in (60) as the Affix Principle (AP).[15]

The independent motivation for the AP may be illustrated with a derivation in which Hop C applies. Given a structure such as that in (61a), Hop C yields a structure such as that in (61b):

(61) (a) . . . [John][PAST][have + EN]$[_V \Delta]$ . . .

(b) . . . [John][[have] PAST]$[_V [_V \Delta]$ EN] . . .

The morpheme EN does not, of course, itself have phonological shape. There are, rather, rules of allomorphy that determine what phonological shape should be inserted into that position, depending on the nature of the stem. The AP explains, quite neatly, why no phonologically realized element can be inserted into the position held by EN in (61b). This has the nice empirical effect of removing any difficulty in deriving such sentences as "Bill hadn't left, but John had," whose second part has the structure given in (61b), while avoiding the impossible string ". . . but John had en."

A treatment of Case morphemes such as that presented by Siegel (1974) provides a similar illustration. Siegel argues that the Possessive Case marker (POSS) "spells out" after the application of certain syntactic rules; a structure such as (62) is the input to a Case realization rule, in her theory, which will produce the NP "Jack's."

(62) $[_{N^4} [_{N^3}$ Jack] POSS]

$$(63) \ [_{N^4} [_{N^3} \ e] \ POSS]$$

Given an input such as (63), however, the Case realization rule must be blocked; it is the AP that does this.

Because of the usefulness of AP in explaining why EN in (61) cannot spell out, I conclude that AP is a filter that follows Hop C. It would, on this account, be an output condition of the core movement rule of inflectional morphology.

If the PH and AP are assumed, we are led to a partial reformulation of the first derivation above, and a resolution of the difficulties raised by the generation of the ungrammatical (52). The first derivation will now include an application of Prefixation;[16] after *wh*-Movement, lexical insertion, and Prefixation, (64) will be produced:

$$(64) \ [_{NP} [_{NP} \ a \ pen]_{\overline{S}} [_S [_{NP} [_{SPEC} \ \begin{bmatrix} -THAT \\ -WH \end{bmatrix} \ [_{NP} \ e]][_{NP} \ John]]$$
$$[wh]$$

to write with $[_{NP} \ e]]]]$
$[wh]$

wh-Insertion and *for*-Insertion may apply to (64). We now note that the derivations in which *wh*-Insertion precedes *for*-Insertion proceed as in (65); as (66) shows, if *for*-Insertion applies first to the subject NP in (64), *wh*-Insertion cannot apply.

(65) *wh*-Insertion $\quad [_{NP} [_{SPEC} \ \begin{bmatrix} -THAT \\ -WH \end{bmatrix} \ [_{NP} \ which]][_{NP} \ John]]$
$[wh]$

$\quad\quad$ *for*-Insertion $\quad [_{NP} [_{SPEC} \ \begin{bmatrix} -THAT \\ -WH \end{bmatrix} \ for][_{NP} \ John]]$

(66) *for*-Insertion $\quad [_{NP} [_{SPEC} \ \begin{bmatrix} -THAT \\ -WH \end{bmatrix} \ for][_{NP} \ John]]$

Therefore, no ordering between these applications need be stated in the grammar.

Turning to the second derivation, note that after *wh-*Movement, Prefixation, and lexical insertion have applied, (67) is produced:

(67) $[_{NP}[_{NP}$ a pen$]_{\overline{S}}[_S[_{NP}[_{SPEC}$ $[_{NP}$ e$]][_{NP}$ e$]]$
$\begin{bmatrix} -\text{THAT} \\ -\text{WH} \end{bmatrix}$ [wh]

to write with $[_{NP}$ e$]]]]$
[wh]

In accordance with the AP, no insertion rule may fill the *e* in SPEC, as desired. The ungrammaticality of (68a) and (68b) is explained.

(68) (a) *a pen for to write with
(b) *a pen which to write with

We may now continue our analysis of relative infinitivals with an examination of NPs such as "a pen with which to write," in which the preposition has been fronted.

Before we begin, however, we must digress for a moment to consider the properties of Case assignment within the assumptions concerning complementizers developed here.

Recall that in Chapter 2 it was proposed that the complementizers, analyzed as SPEC of S, assign Case. We may now go into more detail. We have divided the category SPEC of S into two subclassifications, [+THAT] and [−THAT]. The [+THAT] SPEC is associated with those Ss whose subjects are [−Oblique] (Nominative); the [−THAT] SPEC will be associated with those Ss whose subjects are [+Oblique]. The terminal elements of the [+THAT] SPEC are various:

(69) (a) I believe $\left\{\begin{matrix} \text{that} \\ \emptyset \end{matrix}\right\}$ he left

(b) I know what he did
(c) I know to whom he talked

(d) I don't know $\left\{\begin{matrix} \text{how} \\ \text{whether} \\ \text{when} \\ \text{why} \end{matrix}\right\}$ he did that

Consequently, we assume that an NP *determined* (in the

sense developed in Chapter 2) by

$$[_{\substack{\text{SPEC} \\ [+\text{THAT}]}} \quad \cdots]$$

is assigned [−Oblique], which is realized as Nominative in sentential structures.

Of interest here is the fact that the terminal element of a [+THAT] SPEC need not be mentioned in the assignment of Case. The assignment of [+Oblique] Case apparently depends, as will be seen, on the presence of

$$[_{\substack{\text{SPEC} \\ [-\text{THAT}]}} \quad \text{FOR}]$$

where FOR is the morpheme of which *for* and ∅ are allomorphs. It is likely that it is no accident that the complementizer FOR and the preposition "for" both assign [+Oblique], but an explanation for this fact is lacking.

Assuming this system, we may return to the examples with which we started:

(70) (a) *a pen which him to write with
　　 (b) 　a pen for him to write with
　　 (c) *a pen with which him to write

We note that, given the system of Case assignment presented, precisely the correct predictions are made by the *N Filter. Since only an allomorph of FOR in a [−THAT] SPEC assigns Case, only (70b) will be allowed, as desired. We will return below to the problem of ruling out (71):

(71) *a pen ∅ him to write with

We are now prepared to return to the examples in which the subject of the relative infinitival is not lexically realized.

Recall that the AP explains why both *"a pen for to write with" and *"a pen which to write with" are ungrammatical, while allowing "a pen to write with." The question to be raised is why "a pen with which to write" is allowed.

The answer is contained in the rule of Prefixation itself; "with which" is not itself a grammatical formative. "Which," of course, is a grammatical formative and must prefix when it occurs in a [−THAT] SPEC, as *"a pen which to write with" attests. The problem concerning how to distinguish this example from [+THAT] relatives such as "a pen which wrote well" is treated below.

To complete this discussion of relative infinitivals, we note that the *N Filter accounts for the ungrammaticality of (72a), since "John" will not receive Case, while (72b), in which "with which" is replaced by "for," is the result of unrecoverable deletion.

(72) (a) *a pen with which John to write
(b) *a pen for John to write

We have now achieved the goal of this section—an explanation of the behavior of complementizers in relative infinitivals. We may now examine the implications of the metatheoretical proposals made for a wider range of data.

THAT, FOR, and ∅ Complements

∅-Allomorphy

We may now turn to consider the apparent deletion of the complementizers *that* and *for*. Though data such as those that will be considered are usually described in terms of complementizer deletion, the problem then being to state the structural conditions on the application or output of this rule, the approach adopted here will be rather different. I assume that the complementizers THAT and FOR[17] both have ∅-allomorphs; from this point of view the problem of stating the structural conditions on the deletion of complementizers transposes into the problem of specifying conditions on allomorphic variation. While these theories might appear to be empirically equivalent options, there are a few considerations that suggest that the latter approach is more appropriate. These considerations will be presented after the data have been discussed.

The reanalysis of rules such as complementizer deletion as rules specifying the distribution of ∅-allomorphs has interesting implications for what has traditionally been viewed as a problem in defining the notion "recoverability of deletion." Within a traditional theory of deletion, the operation is allowed under two circumstances: if the deleted element is nondistinct from another element in the sentence, or if the element belongs to the class of "designated elements." The principles governing membership in this last class have remained obscure; however, it appears to be the case that grammatical (as opposed to lexical) formatives, such as complementizers, certain prepositions, case endings, auxiliaries, and so on, are subject to deletion as designated elements, whereas lexical formatives belonging to the major lexical categories are not. This division may be explained if we drop the operation of deletion (in particular, deletion of designated elements) from the theory of grammar altogether; the fact that lexical formatives do not "delete as designated elements" would follow, in the proposed theory, from the observation that lexical formatives, unlike grammatical formatives, lack $\emptyset$-allomorphs. Thus the theory of "what can be deleted as a designated element" transposes into a theory of "what can have a $\emptyset$-allomorph," a theory that explains the observed contrast between grammatical and lexical formatives. With these introductory remarks, we may now consider the distribution of $\emptyset$-allomorph complementizers in standard English.

Assuming a version of the theory of the feature composition of nodes presented in Chomsky (1970), the following generalization can be made:

(73) The non-$\emptyset$ allomorph of the complementizer THAT must appear in the context:

$$\ldots \; [_\alpha \; X] \underline{\qquad} \ldots$$

where $\alpha = [-N, -V]$

The following are representative data from which this generalization can be derived (I assume that adverbs belong to the category $[-N, -V]$):

(74) (a) He is happy [$\emptyset$ [you]] left town $\quad (\begin{bmatrix} +N \\ +V \end{bmatrix} \underline{\quad})$

(b) He told Bill [$\emptyset$ [you]] were

leaving town $\quad (\begin{bmatrix} +N \\ -V \end{bmatrix} \underline{\quad})$

(c) He knows [∅ [you]] left town $\left(\begin{bmatrix} -N \\ +V \end{bmatrix}\_\_\_\right)$

(d) *He believes very strongly

[∅ [you]] left $\left(\begin{bmatrix} -N \\ -V \end{bmatrix}\_\_\_\right)$

Interestingly, the constituent immediately preceding the ∅-allomorph must itself be phonologically realized:

(75) (a) *How happy is John [$_{AP}$ e] ∅ Bill left town

(b) *Who did you tell [$_{NP}$ e] ∅ Bill was leaving town

(c) *John thinks ∅ he is a spy, and Max [$_V$ Δ] ∅ he

is not a spy

In each case, if the ∅-allomorph of THAT following the phonologically null element is replaced by *that*, the examples become grammatical. Consequently, (73) must be amended to (76):

(76) The non-∅ allomorph of the complementizer THAT must appear in the context:

. . . [$_\alpha$ X] ___ . . .

where (i) α = [−N, −V]
or (ii) X is phonologically null

The conditions on the ∅-allomorph of FOR are similar in form, but more severe:

(77) (a) *He would be happy [∅ [you]] to

leave town $\left(\begin{bmatrix} +N \\ +V \end{bmatrix}\_\_\_\right)$

(b) *He encouraged the police [∅ [there]] to

be an investigation $\left(\begin{bmatrix} +N \\ -V \end{bmatrix}\_\_\_\right)$[18]

(c) He wants [∅ [you]] to leave town $\left(\begin{bmatrix} -N \\ +V \end{bmatrix}\_\_\_\right)$

(d) *He wants very much [∅ [there]] to

be an investigation $\left(\begin{bmatrix} -N \\ -V \end{bmatrix}\_\_\_\right)$

As before, the presence of a preceding non-null element is crucial:

> (78) *Max wants [∅ [you]] to leave town,
>
>   and Bill [$_V$ Δ][∅ [you]] to stay

We may now state (79) as a condition on the allomorphy of the complementizers THAT and FOR (note that (79iii) gives us an explanation for the impossibility of (71)):

> (79) The non-∅ allomorph of a complementizer C must appear in the context:
>
> . . . [$_\alpha$ X] ___ . . .
>
> where (i) α = [−N, −V]
> or (ii) X is phonologically null
> or (iii) C = FOR, and α = [+N]

Given (79) as a general statement of the distribution of the complementizers FOR and THAT and their ∅-allomorphs, the possibility of explaining parts of the distributional pattern by means of more general considerations relating to the patterning of ∅-allomorphs can be raised.

Let us begin by examining (79ii). Recall first that what AP expresses is that among the possible PR structures, those in (80) are included, but those in (81) are not, where *M* is a phonologically realized morpheme.

> (80) (a) [∅ [M]]   (b) [[M] ∅]
>
> (81) (a) *[M [∅]]   (b) *[[∅] M]

AP also restricts the distribution of other phonologically unrealized elements—Δ and *e*, for example. Restricting attention to ∅, however, we may make the following claim:

> (82) All ∅-allomorphs must be bound[19]

We may assume that (82) is expressed at a level of representation following Hop C, presumably PR.

Accepting (82), it follows that the structure of (83) is as in (84a), not (84b):

> (83) I think he left

(84) (a) I think $[_{\bar{S}}[_S[\emptyset\ [he]]\ left]]$

    (b) I think $[_{\bar{S}}[\emptyset][_S\ he\ left]]$

And, in particular, it follows that we may narrow our attention to situations in which (79ii) marks as ungrammatical strings of the form (85), where X is null, and where Y contains no terminal elements:

(85) . . . $[_\alpha\ X]\ Y\ [\emptyset\ [M]]$ . . .

Note that we may strengthen the theory in the following way:

(86) Given . . . $Z\ [\emptyset\ [M]]$ . . . , Z must contain $W\ [_\alpha\ X]\ Y$,

    where X is not null, and Y contains no terminal elements

Note that if (86) is adopted, as well as (82), it follows that cases such as those in (87) and (88) may be subsumed under the same generalizations as (75) and (79).

(87) *$[\emptyset\ [he]]$ left is surprising

(88) *$[\emptyset\ [him]]$ to leave would be surprising

It seems clear that the parameters of (86) must be fixed carefully. On the one hand, structures such as (89) must be allowed:

(89) $[\emptyset\ [Men]]$ are fools (where $\emptyset$ is the null determiner)

On the other hand, the distribution of the enclitic, reduced forms of "is," "have," and so on, appears to be constrained by a principle analogous to that expressed in (86):

(90) (a) *John is taller than $[[Fred]\ s][\Delta]$
    (b) *John has more bills than $[[I]\ ve][\Delta]$

Although the similarities seem only suggestive, the generalization expressed in (79ii) appears to be part of a broader pattern in the allomorphy of reduced forms.[20]

Turning now to (79iii), we notice that it (in conjunction with (79i)) effectively restricts the $\emptyset$-allomorph of FOR to strings of the form:

$$(91) \ldots V[\emptyset \ [X]] \ldots$$

It should be pointed out that strings such as (91) are unusual. Most verbs pattern with "arrange," not "want":

(92) (a) I arranged $\left\{ \begin{matrix} \text{for} \\ *\emptyset \end{matrix} \right\}$ Bill to leave

(b) I want $\left\{ \begin{matrix} \text{(very much) for Bill} \\ [\emptyset \ [\text{Bill}]] \end{matrix} \right\}$ to leave

Verbs that do not allow the $\emptyset$-allomorph include the following (considerable idiolectal variation exists, it should be stressed):

(93) afford, agree, aim, appeal, argue, arrange, ask, beckon, beg, consent, contract, contrive, cry (out), decide, demand, desire, endeavor, entail, hint, itch, mean, mind, motion, move, opt, petition, plan, plead, pray, propose, provide, radio, recommend, see fit, signal, telephone, telegraph, vote, wait, watch, wire, wish, write, yearn[21]

The class of verbs like "want" is much more restricted, including the following:

(94) intend, like, prefer, urge, want, expect

Thus (79iii) (in conjunction with (79i)) may be reduced to the statement that there is a morphological rule that allows the $\emptyset$-allomorph of FOR only in the context (95), where V' is a member of the list in (94).

$$(95) \ldots V' \underline{\quad\quad} \ldots$$

V' might be extended to include verbs like "believe," which behaves in a manner parallel to "want" in the relevant respects, although "believe" does not allow "for." I have no positive evidence for this proposal, however.

(96) *I $\left\{ \begin{matrix} \text{want very much} \\ \text{believe very strongly} \end{matrix} \right\}$ $\emptyset$ Max to be on time

The apparently limited observation that infinitival $\emptyset$-complementizers are inserted only in contexts in which they are adjacent to the verb that selects them seems appropriately expressed by this rule of allomorphic conditioning; the general rule appears to be that only *for*, not $\emptyset$, is allowed. Thus (79iii) seems to be limited to these rather exceptional cases.

Trace and "PRO" Subjects

Since it appears that certain morphemes (for example, $\emptyset$) are constrained so as to appear only as bound morphemes, there is an option involved with respect to whether Prefixation is stated as applying obligatorily or optionally. On the one hand, if Prefixation is obligatory, strings of the form (97) may be ruled out since the rule's structural description was met and did not apply.

$$(97) \ . \ . \ . \ [_{\text{SPEC}} \text{M}][[\text{X}] \ . \ . \ .] \ . \ . \ .$$

On the other hand, if the morpheme M is specified in the lexicon (or by some general principle) as being only bound at the level of PR, the stipulation of obligatoriness would be superfluous in ruling out the structure.

Given this option, we choose an optional Prefixation rule, since the existence of stipulations of the bound/free distinction are independently necessary. Below, we will see empirical cause for this choice. Accepting this alternative means that the grammar of standard English must state that the complementizers THAT, FOR, and $\emptyset$ are bound morphemes. On this analysis, a structure such as (98a) will not be derivable; (98b), on the other hand, will be allowed.

(98) (a) He said $[_{\bar{S}}[_{\text{SPEC}}$ that][freedom was everything]]

    (b) He said $[_{\bar{S}}[_{S}[$that [freedom]] was everything]]

Viewing the situation from this perspective, the impossibility of examples such as those in (99) and (100) can be explained.

(99) (a) *Who do you believe that $[_{\text{NP}}$ e] saw Fred

    (b) *Who do you want very much for $[_{\text{NP}}$ e] to hit Fred

(100) *I want very much for $[_{\text{NP}}$ e] to see Fred

Assuming optional Prefixation, and taking (99) as an example, only (101a) and (101b) can be generated as output structures:

(101) (a) . . . $[_{\bar{S}}[_{SPEC}$ that$][_S[_{NP}$ e$] . . .]] . . .$

(b) . . . $[_{\bar{S}}'[_S[_{NP}[_{SPEC}$ that$][_{NP}$ e$]] . . .]] . . .$

The impossibility of (101a) follows from the fact that "that" is a bound morpheme; the impossibility of (101b) follows from AP.

We are at a point now where we must be more precise concerning the notions "bound" and "free" as they apply to morphological structure.

Two notions must be distinguished. On the one hand, I will wish to refer to bound and free occurrences of a morpheme. Given a structure $[_\alpha \gamma[_\beta \delta]]$ (or $[_\alpha[_\beta \delta]\gamma]$), I will say that γ constitutes a bound occurrence of a morpheme just in case γ is an affix of α. A morpheme will constitute a free occurrence just in case it is not contained in another morphological structure. I assume that the distinction between a stem and an affix can be defined structurally, evidence for the proper formulation coming from the phonological component on the one hand and the theory of the lexicon on the other. This is, I believe, a widely held view on this topic.

As to the notions "intrinsically bound" and "intrinsically free," we will say that a morpheme is "intrinsically bound" if it has no free occurrence at PR, and "intrinsically free" if it has no bound occurrence at PR. Some morphemes will be neither intrinsically bound nor intrinsically free; they might have either bound or free occurrences.

The generalizations I wish to state, given this terminology, are that all $\emptyset$-morphemes, as well as all allomorphs of FOR and THAT, are intrinsically bound. We therefore alter (82) to (102):

(102) All $\emptyset$-allomorphs are intrinsically bound

We have also made use of the hypothesis that all SPECs that are [−THAT] are intrinsically bound if they contain only a single grammatical formative; this distinguished *"a pen which to write with" from "a pen with which to write."

It is of interest in this connection to contrast the situation in English with that of French, which, as pointed out in Kayne (1975) and Chomsky and Lasnik (1977), has the following contrast:

(103) (a) *Qui crois-tu qu'a vu Jean
     (b) Qui crois-tu qui a vu Jean

The contrast in (103) is exactly as one would predict, given AP. That *Qui?*, not *Que?*, is a possible single word utterance suggests that *que*, but not *qui*, is intrinsically bound. The deletion of schwa in the morpheme *que* occurs in some bound occurrences of that morpheme. Thus *que* is like the standard English "that" with respect to movement from subject position, as PH and AP together require. This analysis appears to enjoy a slight advantage over that offered in Chomsky and Lasnik (1977), where it is proposed that if *qui* and *que* have different feature contents, differing in at least one feature, *que*, but not *qui*, may be made subject to the filter (104):[22]

(104) $*[_{\bar{S}}$ that $[_{NP}$ e] . . .], unless $\bar{S}$ or its trace is

in the context: $[_{NP}$ NP ___ . . .]

While this proposal is successful, it would be equally available if the grammaticality judgments in (103) were reversed. Within the present framework, however, such a situation would constitute counter-evidence given the usual syntactic analysis of such structures.

A situation that is similar in some respects is noted by Maling and Zaenen (1978). They provide data from Dutch and Icelandic which appear to violate Chomsky and Lasnik's filter. Some of the Dutch facts are given in (105), and some of the Icelandic facts in (106):[23]

(105) (a) Dat is iemand die ik denk dat _____ nog lang hier
      that is someone who I think that _____ yet long here
      zal blijven
      shall stay
      "That is someone who I think will stay here a long time yet"

(b) Wie zei je dat _____ die appel opgegeten heeft
who said you that _____ this apple eaten has
"Who did you say ate this apple"

(106) (a) Það er Olafur, sem Þeir segja að _____ muni koma
it is Olaf that they say that _____ would come
"It is Olaf whom they say would come"

(b) Hvaða bragð sagði hann að _____ vaeri gagnslaust
which maneuver said he that _____ was useless
"Which maneuver did he say was useless"

Of relevance to our proposals here is the observation of Maling and Zaenen that *dat* can never be deleted in Dutch and that the deletion of *að* in Icelandic is only "marginally possible." Translating this observation into our own terms, it is to be interpreted as stating that *dat* and *að* lack Ø-allomorphs. But this would be as expected if *dat* and *að* are not intrinsically bound morphemes. Therefore, the examples in (105) and (106) are as the theory presented here would predict.[24]

I conclude that the theory presented here provides a straightforward account of complementizer allomorphy in the position preceding trace or PRO. The observed contrasts between English, on the one hand, and languages such as Dutch and Icelandic, on the other, are as the theory presented here predicts.

Tensed Relative Clauses

It appears that within any theory of the distribution of complementizers, it is necessary to distinguish relative clause structures from object complement constructions, since there are contrasts such as the following where the embedded subject undergoes *wh*-Movement:

(107) (a) *Who do you believe that [$_{NP}$ e] saw Mary

(b) I arrested the man that [$_{NP}$ e] saw Mary

If, furthermore, the complementizer is not phonologically realized, the pattern of grammaticality is reversed:

(108) (a) Who do you believe [$_{NP}$ e] saw Mary

(b) *I arrested the man [$_{NP}$ e] saw Mary

A second contrast involves restrictive and nonrestrictive relative clauses with respect to complementizer choice:

(109) (a) The man $\begin{Bmatrix} \text{who} \\ \text{that} \\ \emptyset \end{Bmatrix}$ they arrested was innocent

(b) Smith, $\begin{Bmatrix} \text{who} \\ \text{*that} \\ \text{*}\emptyset \end{Bmatrix}$ they arrested, was innocent

Focusing on the status of the complementizer THAT in restrictive relatives, we note that, given the assumptions made so far, either it is not an intrinsically bound morpheme (unlike THAT of complement Ss), or AP must be revised. The structure of (107) apparently can only be as in (110a) or (110b), yet (110a) is ruled out on the assumption that THAT only has bound morpheme status, and (110b) is ruled out by AP.

(110) (a) . . . $[_{\bar{S}}[_{SPEC}$ that$]\!]_S$ . . .

(b) . . . $[_{\bar{S}}[_S[_{NP}[_{SPEC}$ that$][_{NP}$ e$]\!]$ . . .

It would appear that the appropriate extension of the theory so far developed is to postulate that the THAT of restrictive relatives can have free occurrences. Putting aside for a moment the justification for this assumption, we may note that if the relative THAT, like the complement THAT complementizer, has a $\emptyset$-allomorph, and the *wh*-words do not, the simple prohibition against relative THAT in non-restrictives will suffice to explain the contrast between (109a) and (109b).

Consider now the paradigm in (111).

(111) The man $\begin{Bmatrix} \text{who} \\ \text{that} \\ \text{*}\emptyset \end{Bmatrix}$ [$_{NP}$ e] left was innocent

(112) . . . $[_{\bar{S}}[_{SPEC} \atop [+WH]} \begin{Bmatrix} \text{who} \\ \text{that} \\ \text{*}\emptyset \end{Bmatrix}]\!]_S$ . . .

If we assume that the structure of (111) is as in (112), the ungrammaticality of the $\emptyset$-variant follows from the principle that all $\emptyset$-allomorphs are intrinsically bound.

Turning now to the status of THAT$_{rel}$ as a free morpheme, we note first that there are certain relative clause structures in which THAT is the only complementizer allowed:

(113) (a) You can do anything $\begin{Bmatrix} \text{*which} \\ \text{that} \\ \emptyset \end{Bmatrix}$ you want to do

    (b) Nothing $\begin{Bmatrix} \text{*which} \\ \text{that} \\ \emptyset \end{Bmatrix}$ I've seen convinces me

    (c) He discounted what progress $\begin{Bmatrix} \text{*which} \\ \text{that} \\ \emptyset \end{Bmatrix}$ we had made

The dependence between the head of the relative clauses in (113) and the morpheme THAT suggests that THAT behaves as a *wh*-word in these expressions. Although there is a dependence between the head of factive complements, for example, and its complementizer, as is illustrated in (114), the dependence is similar in type to that which obtains between a verb and the complementizer of its complement.

(114) (a) his desire for Max to leave
    (b) his desire that Max leave
    (c) *his desire that Max leaves

In the examples in (113), however, the dependence appears to involve quite different parameters. In particular, THAT$_{rel}$ appears to act as the *wh*-word selected by heads that have certain quantificational properties, though what these properties are is still poorly understood.

Though not without its own difficulties, it is an attractive hypothesis to explore that THAT$_{rel}$ is the suppletive form for "what" in restrictive relative clauses. As is well known, "what" is not allowed in relatives, as (115) indicates:

(115) (a) *You can do anything what you want to
    (b) *The topic what I talked about was affixes

There are, furthermore, certain restricted environments in

which "what" and "that" alternate:

(116) I don't know but $\begin{Bmatrix} \text{what} \\ \text{that} \end{Bmatrix}$ you will reject this

A problem with this analysis is that THAT_{rel} may never be preceded by a preposition, while "what," in indirect questions, for example, marginally allows this:

(117) (a)   I don't know to what you are referring
(b) *The man to that I talked was innocent

A possible resolution of this problem takes the following form.[25] Suppose that THAT_{rel} is indeed to be analyzed as a *wh*-word, though not necessarily a suppletive form of "what," which can replace *e* in the structure (118).

(118) $[_S[_{SPEC} \quad [_{NP} \ e]][_S \cdots]]$
$\begin{bmatrix} +\text{THAT} \\ -\text{WH} \end{bmatrix}$ [wh]

THAT_{rel}, like other *wh*-words, will not have a $\emptyset$-allomorph; in fact, there is the possibility of prohibiting all $\emptyset$-allomorph phrasal categories, but I will not pursue that possibility here. We may assign "the man that *e* left" the structure in (118); NPs such as THAT_{rel}, "who," and so on are not, apparently, intrinsically bound. The string *"the man *e* *e* left" will be prevented if it is stipulated that [+THAT] *wh*-NPs must undergo lexical insertion.[26] The example "who do you believe is crazy" may have *e* in the lower complementizer, since there is no *wh*-NP in that position.

What of "the man Mary saw"? The structure after the insertion of THAT_{rel} ("who" and "which" are alternatives) will be as in (119):

(119) the man $[_S[_{SPEC} \quad [_{NP} \ \text{that}]][_S \ \text{Mary saw } e]]$
$\begin{bmatrix} +\text{THAT} \\ -\text{WH} \end{bmatrix}$ [wh]

The complementizer THAT may now insert; either (120a) or (120b) will be the result, depending on the allomorph chosen.

(120) (a) the man $[_S[_{SPEC} \ \text{that}][_S \ \text{Mary saw } e]]$

(b) the man $[_{\bar{S}}[_{SPEC} \emptyset][_{S}$ Mary saw e]]

Since the allomorphs of THAT are intrinsically bound, Pre-fixation will yield the only grammatical outputs.

What if the complementizer THAT is inserted in the string "the man $[_{NP}$ that$_{rel}]$ e left"? (121a) and (121b) are the possibilities.

(121) (a) the man $[_{\bar{S}}[_{SPEC}$ that$][_{S} [_{NP}$ e] left]]

(b) the man $[_{\bar{S}}[_{SPEC} \emptyset][_{S} [_{NP}$ e] left]]

In (121a), Prefixation will result in a violation of AP; in (121b), Prefixation will yield the structure . . . $[\emptyset [e]]$ . . . , which, if allowed, raises our original problem again.

Suppose, then, that we alter the AP in the following way:

(122) *. . . $[_{\alpha} \gamma[_{\beta} \delta]]$ . . . (or . . . $[_{\alpha}[_{\beta} \delta] \gamma]$ . . .)

where (i) γ is affixed to δ
and (ii) δ is a phonologically unrealized element
unless γ is a phonologically unrealized element of
the same type as δ

The types of phonologically unrealized elements will include e and $\emptyset$. Given this refinement in (122), structures such as $[\emptyset [\emptyset]]$, and $[e [e]]$ will be allowed, but not $[e [\emptyset]]$, $[\emptyset [e]]$, and so forth, as desired.

"Than" and "As" Clauses

If "than" and "as" are assigned the status of morphemes that are not intrinsically bound, the analysis of comparative clauses follows naturally within the framework developed here. "As" and "than," like the *wh*-words, may precede a phonologically unrealized subject, as the following ex-amples indicate:

(123) (a) More people left than $[_{NP}$ e] stayed

(b) As many people left as $[_{NP}$ e] stayed

It is unclear what category, if any, the elements "than" and "as" belong to. What is clear is that their insertion is

linked to the presence of preceding comparative morphemes. The appearance of "than" requires a preceding
-*er*-form; "as" requires a preceding "as," normally.

If the assumption is made that "than" and "as" belong to
the category [+THAT, −WH] SPEC, as in relative clauses,
and if it is assumed that comparatives involve an application
of *wh*-Movement, as is argued in Chomsky (1977), a derivation such as that illustrated in (124) would be allowed:

(124) $\cdots$ $\underset{\overline{S}}{[}\underset{SPEC}{[}$ $e\underset{S}{][}\underset{NP}{[}$ $e]$ $\cdots$
$\begin{bmatrix} +THAT \\ -WH \end{bmatrix}$ [wh]

wh-Movement $\cdots$ $\underset{\overline{S}}{[}\underset{SPEC}{[}$ $\underset{NP}{[}$ $e]]$
$\begin{bmatrix} +THAT \\ -WH \end{bmatrix}$ [wh]

$\underset{S}{[}\underset{NP}{[}$ $e]$ $\cdots$
[wh]

wh-Insertion $\cdots$ $\underset{\overline{S}}{[}\underset{SPEC}{[}$ $\underset{NP}{[}$ who]]
$\begin{bmatrix} +THAT \\ -WH \end{bmatrix}$ [wh]

$\underset{S}{[}\underset{NP}{[}$ $e]$ $\cdots$
[wh]

than-Insertion $\cdots$ $\underset{\overline{S}}{[}\underset{SPEC}{[}$ than$]\underset{S}{][}\underset{NP}{[}$ $e]$ $\cdots$
$\begin{bmatrix} +THAT \\ -WH \end{bmatrix}$ [wh]

The derivation has properties similar to that of the relative
infinitival, the difference being that "than" is not intrinsically bound.

A Note on "Pronoun Deletion"

I will conclude this discussion of the distribution of complementizers with a consideration of the interaction of this
phenomenon with the behavior of Subject-Pronoun Deletion and the insertion (or deletion) of dummy subjects.

Chomsky and Lasnik (1977) restrict their filter (68) with
the condition (71) (their numbering):

(68) *[$_{\overline{S}}$ that [$_{NP}$ e] . . .], unless $\overline{S}$ or its trace is in the context

[$_{NP}$ NP —— . . .]

(71) The filter (68) is valid for all languages that do not have a rule of Subject-Pronoun Deletion, and only these. (Chomsky and Lasnik, 1977, pp. 451–452)

Some such amendment is necessary within their framework; the specific proposal would account, among other things, for the data from Spanish given here:

(125) (Yo) creo que (él) partió

(126) quién tú creiste que [$_{NP}$ e] vio a Juan

Within the framework presented here, the Spanish data follow from the stipulation that *que* in Spanish is not intrinsically bound; Spanish *que* would be like French *qui*, French differing from Spanish in not having a rule of Subject-Pronoun Deletion.

Maling and Zaenen (1978) present data from two dialects of Dutch which suggest, they argue, that (71) should be altered to (2') (their numbering):

(2') Filter (68) is valid for all languages with obligatory dummy subjects, and only these.

The data are, briefly, that (127) and (128) "with *er* are acceptable in all dialects of Dutch; without *er* they are acceptable only in the dialects that allow *er* to be dropped (or not inserted)" (Maling and Zaenen, 1978, p. 482).

(127) Gisteren werkten (er) hier nog veel mensen
yesterday worked (there) here still many people
"Yesterday many people still worked here"

(128) Hij vertelde dat (er) hier gisteren nog veel mensen
he said that (there) here yesterday still many people
werkten
worked
"he said that many people still worked here yesterday"

Further, only in "Dutch A," where the dummy subject is

optional, is (129) allowed; in "Dutch B" dummy subjects are obligatory and (129) is ungrammatical.

(129) Wie zei je dat _____ die appel opgegeten heeft?
      who said you that _____ this apple eaten has
      "who did you say ate this apple?"

Maling and Zaenen argue against Chomsky and Lasnik that the optionality of dummy subjects in Dutch A is not due to their rule of Subject-Pronoun Deletion, but the validity of this argument is not relevant here. What is pertinent is that, within the framework developed in this chapter, we may say that in Dutch B *dat* is intrinsically bound, while in Dutch A it is not. This minimal distinction between the two dialects seems sufficient.[27]

4

Filters on Anaphora Patterns

On the Distribution of Trace at SS

In this chapter an attempt will be made to establish general conditions on membership at the levels of SS and LF, whose application will, effectively, subsume many of those generalizations captured in the framework of Chomsky (for example, 1977c and 1977d). As a point of departure, I wish to quote a few observations from Chomsky which adumbrate, in certain respects, the program developed here:

We might . . . choose to reinterpret SSC [the Specified Subject Condition] as a condition on surface structure interpretation rather than a condition on rules . . .

We might also investigate the possibility of relating this interpretation of SSC to some general prohibition against anaphoric structures of the form (62) rather than the permissible (63), where items with the same subscript are anaphorically related.

$$(62) \ldots X_1 \ldots X_2 \ldots Y_1 \ldots Y_2 \ldots$$
$$(63) \ldots X_1 \ldots X_2 \ldots Y_2 \ldots Y_1 \ldots$$

It is not clear whether such a condition is tenable in general. Consider such examples as (64):

(64) (a) [what books]$_1$ have [those men]$_2$ written t$_1$ about
each other$_2$
   (b) I told them$_1$ [what books]$_2$ PRO$_1$ to read t$_2$
   (c) I$_1$ asked them [what books]$_2$ PRO$_1$ to read t$_2$
   (d) [to whom]$_1$ did John$_2$ seem t$_1$ [t$_2$ to be referring]
   (e) whom$_1$ did you$_2$ ask t$_1$ [what$_3$ PRO$_2$ to read t$_3$]
   (f) Dnes me$_1$ ji$_2$ Jana ukazala t$_1$ t$_2$
today to-him her Jana showed
'Jana showed him to her today.'

But there are many unexplored possibilities, and it may be that
some broader principle is involved. (Chomsky, 1977d, p. 191f.)

Although the conditions developed in this chapter are
formulated differently from those sketched in Chomsky's
generalizations (62) and (63), they incorporate Chomsky's
insight that conditions on anaphora patterns might independently subsume conditions on rules. It will be demon-
strated that at least one theory of anaphora patterns goes a
long way toward achieving explanatory adequacy without
running afoul of examples such as those in Chomsky's (64).

As mentioned at the end of Chapter 3, the analysis of
complementizers developed there requires a radically different conception of what a theory of conditions on anaphora might look like than does the analysis of Chomsky
and Lasnik (1977). It is incumbent on neither analysis, I
should emphasize, to hypothesize that conditions on anaphora patterns be appealed to in order to explain any particular range of phenomena. My point, rather, is that if the
construction of a general theory of anaphora patterns is
taken as a goal, the choice between the treatment of complementizers developed in Chapter 3 and that of Chomsky and
Lasnik (1977) is crucial, in several respects, to the determination of the form of the theory. To illustrate with an obvious
point, it is a question of no small import whether an SS of
the structure of (1) is well formed.

(1) [$_{\overline{S}}$ Who$_1$ [$_S$ do you think [$_{\overline{S}}$ that [$_S$ John saw t$_1$]]]]

The theory of complementizers developed in Chapter 3
yields such structures; in the theory of Chomsky (1977c),
Chomsky and Lasnik (1977), and so on, (1) is not generated,

while (2) is allowed:

(2) $[_{\overline{S}}$ Who$_1$ $[_S$ do you think $[_{\overline{S}}$ t$_1$ that $[_S$ John saw t$_1$]]]]

This difference derives from the fact that in the theory presented in Chapter 3 only one "slot" is allowed in the COMP position, whereas in the theory of Chomsky and Lasnik (1977), two "slots" are required.

Consider, in this light, the Tensed-S Condition of Chomsky (1977c) (the notation S is changed to $\overline{S}$, following current practice):

(3) No rule can involve X, Y (X superior to Y) in the structure

$$\ldots X \ldots [_{\alpha} \ldots Y \ldots] \ldots$$

where Y is not in COMP and α is a tensed $\overline{S}$

Now consider the following filter, which trivially transposes (3) into a condition on anaphora patterns at SS (thus limiting its application to such patterns, but preserving the COMP stipulation):

(4) *$\ldots X_i \ldots [_{\alpha} \ldots Y_i \ldots] \ldots$

where Y is not in COMP and α is a tensed $\overline{S}$

Clearly (2) meets condition (4) while (1) does not—in (1) $Y_i = t_i$, which is within a tensed S but not in COMP. (2) meets the condition, it must be added, only if the plausible assumption is made that the traces "link" in the manner indicated; a linking mechanism seems well motivated in virtually any realization of a program that takes as its goal to establish conditions on anaphora patterns. The point, however, is that the adoption of the theory of complementizers in Chapter 3 leads to contradiction with the filter sketched in (4), whereas the theory of Chomsky and Lasnik (1977) does not. Thus the distinction between (1) and (2) is vital to the proper formulation of a theory of patterns of anaphora.

I will use the term "anaphora" simply to refer to the relation between two nodes whose referential indices are identical. When the term is used in this way, it is clear that there are at least three levels at which filters on anaphora patterns might apply—SS and LF, as well as PR, as discussed in Chapter 2.

The SS anaphora patterns will be due, of course, to the application of movement. Assuming derivations as sketched in (5), it is clear that SS anaphora filters will be relevant to trace anaphora, while LF anaphora filters pertain to reciprocal, reflexive, "PRO," and other similar relations.

(5)

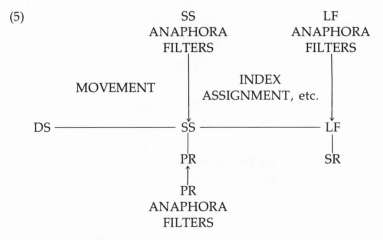

It will be a matter of consequence what level a particular filter applies at.

Some Observations Concerning the Trace of a wh-*Phrase*

Notice first the contrast between the (a) and (b) examples below:[1]

(6) (a) Who saw what
    (b) *What did who see

(7) (a) They know who saw what
    (b) *They know what who saw

In Chomsky (1977c), the following condition, which I will refer to as the Superiority Condition,[2] is suggested to accommodate these and other data; Chomsky notes that, like the A-over-A Condition, it restricts the ambiguity of rule application:

(8) No rule can involve X, Y in the structure

$$\ldots X \ldots [_\alpha \ldots Z \ldots WYV \ldots] \ldots$$

where the rule applies ambiguously to Z and Y
and Z is superior to Y.[3]

Chomsky notes further that, given the underlying structure (9), only (11a), not (11b), may be derived, and given (10), only (12a), not (12b), is allowed, as (8) requires.

(9) John knows what books to give to whom[4]

(10) John knows to whom to give what books[5]

(11) (a) What books does John know to give to whom
  (b) *To whom does John know what books to give

(12) (a) To whom does John know to give what books
  (b) *What books does John know to whom to give

The variants in (9) and (10), as well as those in (13a) and (13b) (from which the identical point can be derived) are allowed, since, by definition, the initial *wh*-phrase in the underlying structure is not superior to the second *wh*-phrase, since, crucially, PP is not a major category.[6]

(13) (a) What did you give to whom
  (b) To whom did you give what

The doublet given in (14a) and (14b) would also apparently be allowed, since, assuming an underlying structure as in (15), the Superiority Condition is inapplicable.

(14) (a) Where did you put what
  (b) What did you put where

(15) You [$_{VP}$ put what where]

Chomsky's characterization of the data is that "*wh*-Movement over a *wh*-phrase P is permissible if P is contained in the predicate phrase . . ." (Chomsky, 1977c, p. 101).

There are, however, certain contrasts in acceptability in the relevant range of data that are not accounted for by condition (8). These contrasts suggest, in fact, a rather different approach.

Consider first (16a) and (16b):

(16) (a) *Who did you give what to
     (b) To whom did you give what

Although the fronting of a preposition with a *wh*-word seldom contributes to grammaticality, in this instance it appears to do so. The following contrasts are of the same type.

(17) (a) *Who did you build what for
     (b) For whom did you build what

(18) (a) *What boxes did you stuff who into
     (b) Into what boxes did you stuff who

(19) (a) *What topic did you tell who about
     (b) About what topic did you tell who

The relevant point about the contrasts in (16) through (19) is that the (a) examples are unambiguously of the form (20); the "stranded" preposition forces this analysis.[7]

$$(20) \ldots [_{[wh]_i} \cdots] \cdots [_{[wh]_j} \cdots]$$
$$\ldots [_{[wh]_i} \cdots] \cdots , i \neq j$$

The (b) examples could as easily be of the form (21), however, if the order of the prepositional phrases in these structures is free.[8]

$$(21) \ldots [_{[wh]_i} \cdots] \cdots [_{[wh]_i} \cdots]$$
$$\ldots [_{[wh]_j} \cdots] \cdots , i \neq j$$

The point, then, is that while the Priority Filter introduced in Chapter 2 correctly predicts that the (a) examples of (16) through (19) are ungrammatical, the Superiority Condition does not predict this.

Since it is the purpose of this chapter to pursue the implications of the hypothesis that only conditions on the well-formedness of members of a level of representation are allowed, not conditions on application, we will adopt (22) as a special case of the Priority Filter applying at PR, and return to Chomsky's condition (8) to examine the empirical differ-

ences between the condition on application, as he formulated it, and (22).

$$(22) * \ldots [_{[wh]_i} \ldots] \ldots [_{[wh]_j} \ldots]$$
$$\ldots [_{[wh]_i} \ldots] \ldots , i \neq j$$

Consider first the fact that both (13a) and (13b) are grammatical. On Chomsky's account this poses no problem,
since, in the underlying representation, neither is superior
to the other. On my analysis there is again no problem if
the order of elements in VP is partially free. The underlying
structure of (13a) would be (23a) and of (13b), (23b):

(23) (a) You gave what to whom
(b) You gave to whom what[9]

Similarly, (14a) would have (24a) (or (24a')) as an underlying
structure, while (14b) would have (24b).

(24) (a) You put where what
(a') You where put what (or, Where you put what)
(b) You put what where

Thus in these cases the equality of elements in VP with respect to superiority is balanced by the equal opportunity of
VP elements other than V to be prior.

Consider now sentences in which a *wh*-phrase is within
a PP.

(25) (a) What did you talk to whom about
(b) Who did you talk about what to

It appears that these sentences contrast with the examples
in (26):

(26) (a) *What did you tell who about
(b) *Who did you tell what to

The examples in (25) have the structure in (27a), while those
in (26) are as in (27b):

$$(27) (a) \ldots [_{[wh]_i} \ldots] \ldots [_{PP} P [_{[wh]_j} \ldots]]$$
$$\ldots [_{[wh]_i} e] \ldots$$

(b) . . . $[_{[wh]_i}$ . . .] . . . $[_{[wh]_j}$ . . .]

. . . $[_{[wh]_i}$ e] . . .

The crucial difference appears to be that in (27b) (but not (27a)) the phrase "wh$_j$" c-commands "wh e$_i$."[10] It follows, therefore, that if we stipulate in (22) that each element c-command the following one, the appropriate distinctions can be gained.

Consider, furthermore, the following sentence, which is grammatical:[11]

(28) I know which books which people read

Example (28) has an SS (and PR) as in (29):

(29) I know $[_{\overline{S}}$ [which books]$_i[_S$ [which people]$_j$ read e$_i$]]

(28) is an apparent counterexample, therefore, both to the Priority Filter and the Superiority Condition. The contrast between (30) and (31) suggests that it is the phrase "which people" in the subject position of (28) that is the source of the difficulty:

(30) *I know which books who read
(31) I know what which people read

Since "which books" was fronted by *wh*-Movement, we assume that the entire NP is assigned the feature [wh]. Since "who" in (30) is [wh], (30) has the SS (32), a violation of the Priority Filter.

(32) . . . $[_{wh_i}$ which books] . . . $[_{wh_j}$ who] . . . $[_{wh_i}$ e]

Consider now the case of (31). Since the phrase "which people" has not undergone *wh*-Movement, there is no reason to assume that the phrase is [wh]. (33) might as easily be the surface structure:

(33) . . . $[_{wh_i}$ what] . . . $[[_{wh_k}$ which][people]]

. . . $[_{wh_i}$ e] . . .

Thus we have further motivation for the notion that

c-command plays a role in the statement of the Priority Filter. Lastly, as would now be predicted, the examples of (34) are grammatical, as opposed to (35), which are not.

(34) (a) Who did you introduce which people to
(b) What did you tell which people about

(35) (a) *Who did you introduce who to
(b) *What did you tell who about

Similarly, trivial counterexamples such as those in (36) will now pose no problem:

(36) (a) Who$_i$ did [the man [who$_j$ [e$_j$ smiled]]] like e$_i$
(b) Who$_i$ did [the man [who$_j$ [e$_j$ wondered [who$_k$ [Max knew e$_k$]]]]] talk to e$_i$

A more precise formulation of the Priority Filter may now be attempted.

The Priority Filter and the "Alikeness" Relation

The Priority Filter might be stated most generally as follows:

(37) *. . . X$_i^1$ . . . X$_j^2$ . . . X$_i^3$ . . . ,
where i ≠ j
and X$_i^1$ c-commands X$_j^2$ and X$_j^2$ c-commands X$_i^3$

I intend the symbol X to range over the nonterminal feature matrices. However, unless the elements that the X symbols may range over are appropriately restricted, the filter will, incorrectly, rule out examples such as those cited by Chomsky above, among others. Accordingly, I propose the preliminary requirement that the interpretations of X be "alike" in the following sense. Consider the class (f$_1$, f$_2$, . . . , f$_n$), which is the set of features whose combinations (and projections) yield the feature matrices of the nonterminal nodes. Given this set, let us say that a feature matrix [αF, βG, . . . , γN] is "alike" to another feature matrix if and only if all of the feature specifications in the first are identical to all of the feature specifications of the second, with the exception of indices and features assigned by redundancy rule, as discussed in Chapter 2. Since the insertion of identical indices is effected by rule, the relation "alike" is similar to the nondistinctness relation of Chomsky (1965), but restricted in range to the class of nonterminal feature matrices.

To take a specific example, consider structures such as the following:

(38) (a) $[_{\begin{bmatrix} +N \\ -V \\ wh \end{bmatrix}_i}$ what] did $[_{\begin{bmatrix} +N \\ -V \\ wh \end{bmatrix}_j}$ who] see $[_{\begin{bmatrix} +N \\ -V \\ wh \end{bmatrix}_i}$ e]

(b) $[_{\begin{bmatrix} +N \\ -V \\ wh \end{bmatrix}_i}$ what] did $[_{\begin{bmatrix} +N \\ -V \end{bmatrix}_j}$ John] see $[_{\begin{bmatrix} +N \\ -V \\ wh \end{bmatrix}_i}$ e]

Given the stipulation that the interpretations of X must be alike, (37) will, correctly, rule out (38a) but not (38b). Similarly, Chomsky's examples (64a) through (64e) cited above are allowed if this stipulation is made.

It seems fairly clear that the "alike" relation, as defined, is too strong. Considering an example such as ?"what did he wonder where John put," "what" has the featural composition of a noun, whereas "where" presumably has the featural composition of an adverb. There are, on the other hand, examples such as "what did John know how to do" which might owe their grammaticality to exactly such a featural difference.

Curiously, whether or not the embedded sentence is tensed is a parameter with respect to these data; contrast (39a) with (39b):

(39) (a) What did John know how to do
(b) ?What did John know how Bill did

Reinhart (1976) lists the following as grammatical:

(40) (a) What don't you know when to file
(b) What don't you know how long to boil
(c) What don't you know where to put

The contrast between these examples and their tensed counterparts persists:

(41) (a) ?What don't you know when Bill filed

    (b) ?What don't you know how long Bill boiled
    (c) ?What don't you know where Bill put

Although the facts at hand are of a quite marginal nature, they allow of a fairly suggestive treatment.

Suppose the existence of an optional marked rule of encliticization between DS and SS which yields structures as in (42):

$$(42) \ [_V [_V \ . \ . \ .] \text{COMP}]$$
$$[+\text{WH}]$$

Suppose further that only a certain class of verbs, including "know," "wonder," and a few others, and a certain class of complementizers are subcategorized so as to occur in such structures. Given SS lexical insertion, no global mechanism will be necessary. We will, furthermore, have derived structures that will not be subject to the Priority Filter, at least in a certain range of cases, as desired. A sentence such as "what does John know how to do" will have a structure as in (43), where "how" does not c-command the trace of "what":

$$(43) \ [_i \text{what}] \ . \ . \ . \ [_V [_V \ \text{know}][_j \text{how}]] \ . \ . \ . \ [_i e][_j e]$$

On the other hand, examples such as *"how does John know what to do," under analysis (44), will still fall under the Priority Filter, a result which also seems as desired.

$$(44) \ [_i \text{how}] \ . \ . \ . \ [_V [_V \ \text{know}][_j \text{what}]] \ . \ . \ . \ [_j e][_i e]$$

Recall that we are assuming that Nominative ($[-\text{Obl}]$) Case is assigned by COMP, or, in our terms, the SPEC of S. Consider in this light a structure such as (45):

$$(45) \ [_i \text{what}] \ \text{does John} \ [[\text{know}][_j \text{how}]] \ \text{Bill did} \ [_i e][_j e]$$

Since the encliticization precedes SS, the complementizer will not be in the correct position to assign Case to "Bill"; consequently we explain the relative unacceptability of (45) with respect to (39a) as a violation of the principle that all lexical NPs must receive Case. The derivation of the string in which encliticization does not apply will yield a violation of the Priority Filter, of course.

Notice that (45) is considerably better than (46):

(46) [ᵢwho] does John [ᵥ[ᵥ know][ⱼhow]][ᵢe] did the job [ⱼe]

In this structure it is the trace of "who" that receives no Case. It is not clear to me why a violation due to a quantifier's having no variable (assuming that a variable is a *Cased* trace) should be worse than a violation of the *N Filter applying to "Bill" in (45), but such appears to be the case. The contrast is preserved in (47) and (48), interestingly:

(47) *[ᵢwhat] do you [[know][ⱼhow]] Bill to do [ᵢe][ⱼe]

(48) **[ᵢwho] do you [ᵥ[ᵥ know][ⱼhow]][ᵢe] to do the job [ⱼe]

But at this point, it would appear that the data are hardly firm enough to support theories of any generality; we will assume, however, that the encliticization proposal is correct in its essentials. Notice now that if this is the correct line of explanation, examples such as (39a) and (40a) through (c) are not relevant to the task of fixing the definition of the "alikeness" relation. It is, rather, the fact that (39b) and (41a) through (c) are ungrammatical that is crucial. What these examples apparently show is that sharing the [wh] feature is alone sufficient to engage the Priority Filter. As further evidence for this, consider (49a) and (b), which contrast greatly in grammaticality:

(49) (a) I know who is how tall
     (b) *I know [how tall][who] is

Since (49b) has a structure as in (50), we have a further piece of evidence that the [wh] feature itself can satisfy the "alikeness" relation.

(50) . . . $\left[\begin{smallmatrix} +N \\ +V \\ wh \end{smallmatrix}\right]_i$ how tall$\left]\left[\begin{smallmatrix} +N \\ -V \\ wh \end{smallmatrix}\right]_j$ who$\right]$ . . . $\left[\begin{smallmatrix} +N \\ +V \\ wh \end{smallmatrix}\right]_i$ e$\right]$ . . .

Accordingly, I propose the following refinement of the "alikeness" relation. Let us divide the set of nonterminal features into two classes: one containing the features αN and βV, which *every* lexical element will be dominated by;

the other containing an optional specification of the feature [wh] which will appear only in nodes dominating *wh*-elements. This merely constitutes a formal recognition of an elementary distinction: the features αN and βV are the categories of the PS rules, subcategorization, and so on, while the feature [wh] is a feature associated with particular lexical items and which may "percolate" to nodes that dominate it. Let us call each subset a cell, notating a node as follows:

$$(51) \ [\begin{bmatrix} \alpha N \\ \beta V \end{bmatrix} \ \ldots]$$
$$([\text{wh}])$$

We will call the [wh] cell of a nonterminal feature representation the "designated cell" of the representation; if a representation lacks a [wh] cell, we will call the cell containing αN, βV, the "designated cell."

We may now define the Priority Filter as follows:

(52) Given the structure:
$$\ldots A_i \ldots A_j' \ldots A_i'' \ldots$$
   where (i) A_i c-commands A_j' and A_j' c-commands A_i''
      (ii) A, A', A'' contain alike designated cells
      (iii) $i \neq j$
assign *

A sentence such as "what did John see" will now be given the structure:

$$(53) \ [\begin{bmatrix} +N \\ -V \end{bmatrix} \ \text{what}] \ \text{did} \ [\begin{bmatrix} +N \\ -V \end{bmatrix} \ \text{John}] \ \text{see} \ [\begin{bmatrix} +N \\ -V \end{bmatrix} \ e]$$
$$[\text{wh}]_i \qquad\qquad\qquad\qquad\qquad [\text{wh}]_i$$

Since the designated cells of the three main nodes are [wh], $[+N, -V]$, and [wh], which are not all alike, structure (53) is not ruled out by the Priority Filter. If, however, "John" were replaced by "who," that node would have the designated cell [wh], the designated cells of the three would be "alike," and the structure would be ruled out, as desired.

Having stated the Priority Filter in these very general terms, we see that it seems to be much *too* general. While it appears to make correct predictions when $A'' = e$, it fails when A″ = the reflexive or "each other," for example:

(54) [$_i$John] talked to [$_j$Bill] about [$_i$himself]

(55) [$_i$The men] introduced [$_j$the women] to [$_i$each other]

Recall, however, that at the level of SS (and PR), *only* moved elements and their traces are coindexed; the rule that assigns coindexing in (54) and (55) is part of the component that relates SS and LF, as will be discussed in Chapter 5. Thus, at the level of SS (and PR), (55) has a structure as in (56), and therefore does not violate (52).

(56) [$_i$The men] introduced [$_j$the women] to [$_k$each other]

An explicit but informal statement of the Indexing Rule is given in (57).[12]

(57) Assign the index of "each other" to another NP in the same phrase marker.

Pursuing the implications of (52), we note that the condition still appears to be too general. Consider the following contrast:

(58) (a)   John would be fun to give presents to
     (b) *John was given presents to

If it is assumed that the surface structures of (58a) and (58b) are as in (59a) and (59b), it would appear that the unquestioned grammaticality of (58a) constitutes a counterexample to the Priority Filter, if a Tough-Movement analysis is assumed.

(59) (a)   [$_i$John] would be fun to give [$_j$presents] to [$_i$e]
     (b) *[$_i$John] was given [$_j$presents] to [$_i$e]

Under such an analysis, (60) would be the structure preceding NP-Movement (I assume, of course, that there is not an independently motivated separate rule of Tough-Movement).

(60) It$_k$ would be fun to give [$_j$presents] to [$_i$John]

There are, however, two alternative analyses, that of Chomsky (1977e) and that of Lasnik and Fiengo (1974). In this last analysis, a rule of Object Deletion was proposed; this analysis is, as pointed out in that paper, empirically equivalent to an analysis in which an interpretive rule anaphorically relates the relevant nodes, the second of which would be *e*. Given these assumptions, the SS (and PR) of (59) would be as in (61):

(61) [$_i$John] would be fun to give [$_j$presents] to [$_k$e].

A rule of Index Assignment, similar to (57), would apply to yield the appropriate LF. A similar analysis could be proposed for (62), as mentioned in note 12 (but see the section on the NP Filter contrasted with the Specificity Condition later in the chapter).

(62) John$_i$ promised Bill$_j$ [e$_k$ to leave]

Under these assumptions, neither (61) nor (62) constitutes a counterexample to the Priority Filter.

In the analysis of Chomsky (1977e), (63a) has (63b) as a directly underlying structure:

(63) (a) John is easy (for us) to please

(b) John is easy (for us) [$_{\bar{S}}$[who for] PRO to please t]

The elements "who" and "for" delete in accordance with certain independently motivated output conditions. Of relevance here is the fact that, given such an analysis, the SS (and PR) of (61) would be (64), not (59a):

(64) $\begin{bmatrix} \begin{bmatrix} +N \\ -V \end{bmatrix}_i \text{John} \end{bmatrix}$ would be fun to give

$\begin{bmatrix} \begin{bmatrix} +N \\ -V \end{bmatrix}_j \text{presents} \end{bmatrix}$ to $\begin{bmatrix} \begin{bmatrix} +N \\ -V \end{bmatrix} \text{e} \end{bmatrix}$
$[wh]_k$

(64) does not, of course, violate the Priority Filter, since the trace has a designated [wh] feature, whereas the other NPs do not. The nonterminals of the elements "John" and *e* in (62) are not coindexed in this analysis either, the relation between "John" and the complement being given by the Rule of Predication.[13] Note that if (63b) is held to be the surface structure of (63a), and the "deletions" that yield (63a)

are held to apply in the phonological component, there is still no bar to holding that the Priority Filter applies at the level of SS.

In concluding this section, it must be emphasized that the Priority Filter cannot account for *all* of the "overgenerations" of NP-Movement. As was noted above, the c-command requirement on the Priority Filter allows, among other examples, the following, where *wh*-Movement is the relevant rule:

(65) What$_i$ did you talk to whom$_j$ about e$_i$

Consider, however, the following example, where NP-Movement applies:

(66) *Linguistics$_i$ was talked to John$_j$ about e$_i$

Given the c-command requirement, the Priority Filter will not rule out (66). The ungrammaticality of (66) is due, of course, to the i-set-i Filter, developed in Chapter 2.

More problematic are examples such as (67):

(67) John was taken advantage of

Example (67) could, plausibly, be given a structure as in (68):

(68) [$_{NP_i}$ John] was taken [$_{NP_j}$ advantage][$_{PP}$ of [$_{NP_i}$ e]]

The problem to be faced, therefore, centers on the fact that (67) is grammatical, although (68) appears to satisfy the Priority Filter.

One alternative, which has a good deal of plausibility, is to maintain that example (67) should be assigned a structure as in (69a), or, perhaps, (69b):

(69) (a) [$_{NP_i}$ John] was [$_{AP}$ taken [$_{NP_j}$ advantage]]

[$_{PP}$ of [$_{NP_i}$ e]]

(b) [$_{NP_i}$ John] was [$_{AP}$ taken [$_{NP_j}$ advantage] of][$_{NP_i}$ e]

With respect to the Priority Filter, both (69a) and (69b) have the merit that NP$_j$, "advantage," does not c-command [$_{NP_i}$ e] and, therefore, the Priority Filter is inapplicable.

The proposal that "take advantage (of)" is a constituent gains no support, however, from the observation that it, and other idioms, have "lexical senses." If lexical insertion applies at the level of surface structure, it is clear that provision must be made for discontinuous elements such as "bring NP to," the verb-particle construction (at least as analyzed in Chapter 2), and so on. An example such as (70) brings only weak support to the proposal, being ungainly at best:

(70) (?)a seldom taken advantage of proposal

It appears, therefore, that while (69) may well be the correct analysis of such examples, motivation for it is hard to obtain.

It is worth noting that there are independent data that suggest that "advantage" in (67) is not an NP.

Consider first the examples in (71):

(71) (a) *John was taken unfair advantage of
(b) *John was taken too much advantage of

In these examples, an NP analysis is virtually forced. Consider also the examples in (72):

(72) (a) *John was paid great heed to
(b) *John was kept careful tabs on

These data, taken together, suggest that "advantage," "heed," "tabs," and so on can appear in structures such as either (73) or (74), but not (75):

(73) (a) $[_A$ taken $[_N$ advantage$]$ of$]$ NP[14]

(b) $[_V$ take $[_N$ advantage$]$ of$]$ NP

(74) (a) $[_A$ taken$][_{NP}$ (unfair) advantage$][_{PP}$ of NP$]$

(b) $[_V$ take$][_{NP}$ (unfair) advantage$][_{PP}$ of NP$]$

(75) (a) $[_A$ taken $[_{NP}$ (unfair) advantage$]$ of$]$

(b) $[_V$ take $[_{NP}$ (unfair) advantage$]$ of$]$

The impossibility of (75) would follow from the plausible

morphological generalization that a phrasal category may not be a morphological unit within a lexical category. Structures such as (73) would, of course, be allowed. (67) is assigned (73a), while (71a) could only be assigned (74a), which would occasion a violation of the Priority Filter, as desired.

Of course, if we assume the null hypothesis that NPs such as $[_{NP}$ (unfair) advantage] must be assigned Case, the *N Filter will rule out (71a), if it is analyzed as containing structure (74a). There is another interesting point of detail with respect to the *N Filter that deserves mention here. The sentence "John was taken advantage of" will contain structure (73a) in the analysis presented here, yet plainly "advantage" will not receive Case. Why is this not a violation of the *N Filter?

The answer, plainly, is that the *N Filter may not analyze elements *within* lexical categories. The filter must be stated in such a way that it not require that Ns be Cased which are contained in such lexical items as $[_A [_N$ smoke]$[_A$ filled]], $[_N [_N$ meat]$[_N$ grinder]], $[_V [_N$ horse]$[_V$ whip]], and so on. Apparently the *N Filter analyzes NP *heads*, although there are details of execution here that remain to be worked out. In "advantage was taken of John," "advantage" must be dominated by NP, and Case must be assigned, as desired; a sentence such as *"it is $[_A$ likely] advantage to be taken of John" violates the *N Filter, again as desired.

We may conclude, then, that examples such as "John was taken advantage of" do not constitute violations of the Priority Filter.

The major result of this section is that given the Priority Filter, a quite wide range of *wh*-Movement applications, which, in the framework of Chomsky (1977) are constrained by the Superiority and "*wh*-Island" Conditions, are filtered by a single mechanism. Furthermore, as we have seen, the Priority Filter apparently provides a better account of certain extractions from VP than does the Superiority Condition. We may add this range of data to that provided in Chapter 2 as support for the Priority Filter proposal.

ON THE LEVEL OF APPLICATION OF THE PRIORITY FILTER

We have now extended the range of data that the Priority Filter is to encompass to include not only the outputs of Hop C but *wh*-Movement as well. We may now ask at what level this filter is to apply.

It seems clear that LF is not a possibility. At that level we will wish to have representations such as (76), which is the output of two applications of QR, the quantifier-raising rule of May (1977a).

(76) $[[_{NP_i}$ everyone$][[_{NP_j}$ someone$][[_{NP_i}$ e$]$ saw $[_{NP_j}$ e$]]]]$

We infer that the Priority Filter must apply at either SS or PR.

We know that the Priority Filter must apply at PR to choose among Hop C outputs. The question then is whether PR application is sufficient. It would appear that it is. There is at the moment no evidence for the existence of a rule applying between SS and PR that would disturb the structural relations between *wh*-words. On the other hand, allowing the Priority Filter to apply at SS would appear to pose no difficulty. The falsifiable option open to us, however, is that no filter, taking the Priority Filter as a particular, may apply at more than one level. We accept that option here.

THE PRIORITY FILTER CONTRASTED WITH OPACITY

We must begin by sketching in the relevant properties of the Opacity Condition as developed by Chomsky (1978). We will focus our attention here only on the examples that involve the deletion of the referential indices of NPs. Consider, then, the structure in (77):

(77) $\ldots [_{\beta} \ldots \delta_k \ldots \alpha_i \ldots] \ldots$

Let us assume that β is the minimal node dominating δ_k and α_i and that δ_k is a subject that c-commands α_i. Adopting as a bit of terminology the idea that a node is in the *domain* of another if the latter c-commands it, we may say that α_i is in the *domain* of δ_k. Let us say that α_i is *free*(i) in β if there is no γ in β with index i that c-commands α. Having sketched these notions, we may say that if α: (1) has an index i, (2) is free(i) in β, and (3) is in the domain of the subject of β, then the index i of α is deleted from the designated index of α.[15] This is essentially Chomsky's proposal, as it relates to the facts formerly subsumed under the Specified Subject Condition. Consider its application to example (78):

(78) The men believed $[_\beta$ John$_k$ to hate each other$_i]$

The index of "each other" will delete. It is, however, a property of reciprocals as well as other elements that they must bear the referential index of another NP in the same sentence. The contradiction between these two principles leads to the ungrammaticality of (78).

If the application of the Priority Filter is to be restricted to PR, as the conclusions of the preceding section would suggest, it is clear that the only areas of "overlap" between Opacity and the Priority Filter will have the form (79a) or (b):

(79) (a) $\ldots A_i \ldots A'_j \ldots e_i \ldots$
(b) $\ldots e_i \ldots A'_j \ldots A_i \ldots$
where A'_j is a subject

Since examples such as (79b) are independently ruled out (see Chapter 5),[16] attention focuses on (79a). An example of this form is (80):

(80) *John$_i$ believes Bill$_j$ to like e$_i$

Structure (80) is the output of NP-Movement. After Case Assignment and Indexing, we will have (81):

(81) $[_{NP_i}$ John] believes $[_{NP_{(j,(i))}}$ Bill] to like $[_{NP_{(i,(i,j))}}$ e]

The object of "like" will receive an anaphoric index since it receives Case. The index i in the anaphoric index of $[_{NP}$ e] will delete by Opacity, as occurs in "John believes Bill to like him." We have no overlap here, then, since only the Priority Filter rules out the resulting structure.

Example (82) is somewhat different.

(82) $[_{NP_i}$ John] believes $[_{NP_{(j,(i))}}$ Bill] to be liked $[_{NP_i}$ e]

(82) is the representation after Indexing. After Opacity, the referential index of the trace will delete, leaving the trace improperly bound.

There are, lastly, examples such as (83) in which Opacity alone applies to structures in which the anaphor is e.

(83) For John$_i$ to dislike e$_j$ amused Fred$_j$

We have, then, a narrow area of overlap between the two conditions.

The "Boundedness" of Proper Binding

In Chomsky (1977c), much of the explanatory force of Ross's constraints (1967) is subsumed under the Subjacency Condition, which was formulated as a condition on the application of extraction rules. It may be stated as follows:

(84) No extraction rule may involve X and Y in the structure

$$\ldots X \ldots [_\alpha \ldots [_\beta \ldots Y \ldots$$

where α and β are bounding nodes

It is clear that the condition (84) may not be appealed to in the framework of this book, since it is a condition on application, not on membership at a level. It is necessary, therefore, to devise an explanation for the "island" phenomena which Ross and Chomsky have addressed that is consistent with the metatheory of this volume.

However, the same empirical result, given other subsidiary assumptions, can be obtained with a filter formulated as in (85):

(85) *$\ldots X_i \ldots [_\alpha \ldots [_\beta \ldots e_i \ldots$

where α and β are bounding nodes

The question of the level of application of (85) may be left aside, since it is clear, within the framework developed in this book, that no such filter may be appealed to. An SS such as (86) constitutes a counterexample; the LF of this sentence also violates (85):

(86) Who$_i$ do you believe [that [Max said [that [Fred hates e$_i$]]]]

It would appear to be possible, in principle, within the framework of Chomsky (1977c) and later work of Chomsky and others, to adopt either (84) or (85) as the correct formulation of the Subjacency Condition. Within this approach, (87), not (86), constitutes the SS of the sentence corresponding to (86):

(87) Who$_i$ do you believe [e$_i$ that [Max said [e$_i$ that [Fred hates e$_i$]]]]

(87) does not violate (85) (nor would its derivation violate (84)). The analysis implicit in (87) differs from that adopted in this volume, in particular, in Chapter 3, in that COMP may contain more than one element. This possibility may be formalized either by generating two "slots" under the COMP node, or by proposing that *wh*-words adjoin to the COMP node.

Note that the question as to whether COMP contains two "slots" (or whether *wh*-Movement is an adjunction) is quite independent of the question of the correctness of the successive cyclic theory of the application of *wh*-Movement. The surface structure given in (86) *could* have resulted from successive cyclic application of *wh*-Movement; in that derivation, the insertions of "that" covered e$_i$ in both instances. The point is that the application of *wh*-Movement is totally free; the problem is to guard against its overgeneration through filtering mechanisms. The next section is devoted to this problem.

The NP Filter

An Initial Formulation

In this and the next two sections, I wish to consider the entailments of the proposal that (88) is a filter at SS, but that there is not a Subjacency Condition of the general form (85).

(88) *. . . X$_i$ . . . [$_{NP}$ . . . e$_i$ . . .] . . .

My argument will be that given (88), the Priority Filter, and a few other quite general mechanisms which will be developed, no explanatory force is lost if the Subjacency Condition is dispensed with.

On the Asymmetry of the NP Filter

It seems clear that there do exist structures in which constituents are extracted to the right out of NPs. Extraposition examples are among the most obvious instances:

(89) (a) $[_{NP}$ A review $e_i]$ appeared $[_{PP_i}$ of Bill's book$]^{17}$

(b) $[_{NP}$ A review $e_i]$ appeared $[_{S_i}$ which should

never have been written]

Similarly, the rule Q-Floating extracts Q from NP; in the following sentence, the Q originated inside of the NP, as is argued, for example, in Fiengo and Lasnik (1976).

(90) The girls were all healthy

These examples, then, would seem to be counterexamples to the NP Filter; it would appear that the filter cannot be held to constrain outputs of rightward movement.

Recall, however, that it was argued in Chapter 2 that Q-Floating may in fact be an instance of the general rule Hop C, which applies in the domain relating SS and PR. Since the NP Filter applies at SS, the grammaticality of (90) may not be relevant to the question of the symmetry of the NP Filter. It would be consistent to maintain that the NP Filter applies at SS, is symmetrical, and that Q-Float simply follows the application of that filter.

A similar claim might be made concerning either or both of the examples in (89). This topic will be taken up in the section on the Specificity Condition, where certain contrasts between the NP and Specificity Filters will be discussed. With respect to PP-Extraposition, it appears best to maintain that the operation *precedes* SS. This is so because of the fact that examples such as "what book did a review appear of" are grammatical. If PP-Extraposition followed SS, applying between SS and PR, the NP Filter would rule out such examples. In light of this consideration, (89a) appears to be a genuine counterexample to the claim that the NP Filter is symmetrical. Consequently, I will assume that the NP Filter is not symmetrical.

Chomsky (1977e) uses examples such as that in (89) to argue against the NP Constraint of Bach and Horn (1976). Chomsky's general characterization of extraction from NP is as follows:

(91) In the structure

$$[_{\bar{S}} \text{ COMP } [_S \cdots [_{NP} \cdots Y \cdots] \cdots] \cdots]$$

Y cannot be extracted from S; in particular, *wh*-Movement cannot move Y to COMP.

Chomsky presents an analysis of PP complements in NPs that obviates such apparent counterexamples to (91) as (92):

(92) Who did he see a picture of

He proposes that a Readjustment Rule[18] yields (93b) from (93a); after this application, *wh*-Movement is allowed, to yield such sentences as (92).

(93) (a) He saw $[_{NP}$ a picture of John]

(b) He saw $[_{NP}$ a picture $e_i][_{PP_i}$ of John]

Note that if the Readjustment Rule is formulated as movement, as indicated in (93), we have another argument that a symmetrical version of the NP Filter cannot be maintained. In the section on the Specificity Condition later in this chapter, the possibility is considered that the Readjustment Rule and PP-Extraposition are identical. Here, however, we must return to a consideration of possible *leftward* violations of the NP Filter.

Note, now, that the characterization of extraction given in (91) is narrower than the claim made by (88) with respect to leftward movement. While (88) will rule out (94), (94) is consistent with (91):

(94) $[_{\bar{S}} \text{ COMP } [_S \cdots X_i \cdots [_{NP} \cdots e_i \cdots] \cdots]]$

Chomsky presents an example of the form (94), arguing that the NP Constraint of Bach and Horn (and, in effect, the

NP Filter that I propose) is too strong. While emphasizing the tentative nature of the analysis, Chomsky argues for the existence of a structure as in (95):

(95) $[_{\overline{S}}$ COMP $[_S[$Of the students in the class$]_i$

$[_{NP}$ several $e_i]$ failed the exam$]]$

There are examples, however, that seem to undermine a movement analysis of such structures. Consider the examples in (96).

(96) (a) Of the students in the class, Bill's favorites are intelligent
(b) Of the students in the class, Mary has more potential than Fred

(96a) is problematic, under Chomsky's assumptions, since, if the analysis is as in (97), we have a violation of Opacity.

(97) $[_{\overline{S}}$ COMP $[_S[_i$Of the students in the class$]$

$[_{NP}$ Bill's favorites $e_i]$ are intelligent$]]$

If, on the other hand, the PP does not originate inside of the subject NP, we do not have an output of the form (94). Example (96b) suggests that there must indeed be an alternative source for the initial PPs; no movement from within an NP is plausible, in this case. Thus the argument has not been made that outputs of the form of (94) exist; that they do not is entailed by the NP Filter.

Let us now take stock. We have seen that, while there appear to be clear-cut counterexamples to the NP Filter involving rightward movement, there is no apparent reason not to invoke the NP Filter as a condition on leftward movement outputs.[19]

The NP Filter Contrasted with the Specificity Condition

SOME PRELIMINARY REMARKS
CONCERNING PRO AND TRACE

In this section the NP Filter developed above will be contrasted with the Specificity Condition, an initial version of which will be formulated here. Of primary importance will be the result that the Specificity Condition should apply at LF, while the NP Filter should apply at SS. Diagram (98) summarizes the theory as it will be developed at the end of this section:

(98)

$$
\begin{array}{ccc}
& \text{NP Filter} & \text{Specificity Condition} \\
& \downarrow & \downarrow \\
\text{DS} \text{------} \text{SS}' \text{------} \text{SS} & \text{-----------} & \text{LF} \\
& \downarrow & \downarrow \\
& \text{PR} & \text{SR} \\
& \uparrow & \\
& \text{Priority Filter} &
\end{array}
$$

It is clear that there are well-formed LFs of the shape (99):

(99)   . . . X_i . . . $[_{NP}$ . . . X_i . . .] . . .

The LF corresponding to the example in (100) has such a structure:

(100) The men believe $[_{NP}$ pictures of $\begin{Bmatrix} \text{themselves} \\ \text{each other} \end{Bmatrix}]$

to be on sale

The distribution of the element e differs from the reflexive and reciprocal pronoun, as has already been noted:

(101) (a) *Who$_i$ do you believe $[_{NP}$ pictures of $e_i]$

to be on sale

(b) *The men$_i$ were believed $[_{NP}$ pictures of $e_i]$

to be on sale

A puzzle arises with regard to the status of the element usually referred to as PRO, which is, syntactically, $[_{NP}$ $e]$. If we assume that coindexing at SS arises only through movement, we will have structures such as (102), where the NPs are not coindexed.

(102) The men want $[_{NP}$ $e]$ to leave

Yet if PRO is not coindexed at the level of SS, what is to prevent (103), which is, in all relevant structural respects, parallel to (100)?

(103) The men want [$_{NP}$ pictures of [$_{NP}$ e]] to be on sale

An intriguing possibility to pursue is that *all e* elements that appear at the level of SS are coindexed with other elements in the same phrase marker by convention. Under this account, PRO and trace would receive their indices at the same level of analysis. If this were the case, (103) would pattern with (101), not (100), and would fall under the NP Filter. Coindex would apply to the reciprocal and reflexive pronouns, but not to PRO, in the component relating SS and LF.

It is of interest to note that by establishing two coindexing processes, one yielding coindexing patterns at SS, the other at LF, we may reinterpret NP-Movement and *wh*-Movement as *e*-Coindexing at surface structure, subsuming PRO under this generalization.[20]

Before considering the details of this observation, we must examine two quite specific problems arising from this proposal. First, we have the problem of finding a well-formed derivation for (104). Second, we have the problem of analyzing certain contraction data which, in the most principled account yet formulated, require a contrast between PRO and trace.

(104) John promised Bill [[e] to leave]

There is, in fact, a double problem associated with "promise," given the framework developed here. On the one hand, structure (105), though apparently the correct SS and PR of the sentence, violates the Priority Filter, and on the other, structure (106) must be ruled out, though it is in violation of no principle yet considered.

(105) [$_{NP_i}$ John] promised [$_{NP_j}$ Bill][[$_{NP_i}$ e] to leave]

(106) *[$_{NP_i}$ John] was promised [$_{NP_i}$ e][[$_{NP_i}$ e] to leave]

The double problem admits of a unified solution. Suppose that the lexical verb-adjective pair "promise/promised" is listed as an exception to the Priority Filter in the following manner:

(107) * . . . A_i . . . A_j . . . A_i . . . , where $i \neq j$
except: "promise/promised," where $i = j$

The effect will be, of course, to rule out (106), while allowing (105), as desired. We find, then, that in this marked circumstance, the effect of the Priority Filter is precisely reversed. The unmarked situation, represented by "persuade/persuaded," shows the familiar pattern:

(108) (a) $^*[_{NP_i}$ John] persuaded $[_{NP_j}$ Bill$][[_{NP_i}$ e] to leave]

    (b) $[_{NP_i}$ John] persuaded $[_{NP_j}$ Bill$][[_{NP_j}$ e] to leave]

(109) $[_{NP_i}$ John] was persuaded $[_{NP_i}$ e$][[_{NP_i}$ e] to leave]

The proposal that marked exceptions reverse the effects of a filter is suggestive, I believe, but I will not pursue it here. To conclude, the reader will recall that reflexives and reciprocals will not have received their referential indices at SS, which fact allows (110) with the indices shown:

(110) $[_{NP_i}$ John] promised $[_{NP_j}$ himself$][[_{NP_i}$ e] to leave]

We may now turn to the contraction data. With respect to the phenomena dealt with here, the central relevant data are contained in the following contrast:

(111) (a) Who do you $\begin{Bmatrix} \text{want to} \\ ^*\text{wanna} \end{Bmatrix}$ succeed Teddy

    (b) I $\begin{Bmatrix} \text{want to} \\ \text{wanna} \end{Bmatrix}$ succeed Teddy

Within the formalism developed in Chomsky (1978), (111a) and (b) will have surface structures roughly as in (112a) and (b):

(112) (a) Who$_i$ do you want [$_i$e] to succeed Teddy
    (b) I want [e] to succeed Teddy

Chomsky proposes the convention that $[_\alpha$ e] be automatically deleted in the phonetic interpretive component unless α is indexed. The impossibility of deleting $[_i e]$ in (112a) suffices to block the contraction rule, as is desired.

Since, given my proposal that all e elements are coindexed at the level of SS, the SS of (111a) will not be as in (112a) but as in (113), it is clear that the convention that Chomsky proposes cannot be appealed to.

(113) I_i want $[_i e]$ to succeed Teddy

There is, however, a slightly different formulation of Chomsky's condition that gives the appropriate results.

A different convention is proposed in Chomsky (1978)[21] which states that *wh*-Movement "from S to COMP, by convention, assigns the feature [+COMP] to the trace along with the normal index assigned by the movement rule" (Chomsky, 1978, p. 6). It is this trace that is identified as a variable by the *wh*-Interpretation rule. Suppose we adopt the convention that $[_\alpha e]$ delete in the phonetic interpretive component unless it is indexed [+COMP]. It appears that this yields the same consequences with respect to these data as Chomsky's convention, while allowing PRO to be an indexed e, as is desired in the theory as I have constructed it.

There is, however, a difference between Chomsky's proposal and the one that I have just outlined. In Chomsky's view, any trace, be it from *wh*-Movement or NP-Movement, will block contraction, whereas my own proposal asserts that only traces of *wh*-Movement have that effect. Although the absence of any cases in which contraction applies across an NP-Movement trace would not, technically, falsify the theory I propose, it would considerably strengthen my case, and, correspondingly, weaken Chomsky's, if such a situation could be found. I believe there to be such examples, which I will present directly. I would like first, however, to consider a few such cases that have been presented in the literature.

In Emonds (1977) the following examples are presented; they form part of his argument that Lightfoot (1977) is incorrect in maintaining that traces, but not PROs, block adjunction.

(114) (a) Wilson is certain 'a take this hard
     (b) We just happen 'a like to write on lots of unrelated topics

Emonds takes these examples to be instances of *to*-Adjunction, suggesting that "this process is responsible for, among other things, the loss of the segment *t* of the morpheme *to* after a stop or nasal" (1977, p. 240). I consider the proposed description of the effects of *to*-Adjunction plausible, although it might be denied. If one accepts the proposal, the examples in (114) constitute instances of contraction across the trace of NP-Movement. Emonds also gives (115) as an example:

(115) They were taken 'a see a better doctor

Consider now the following examples, cited by Emonds:

(116) (a) We needa fix this car
     (b) *Three hours we'll needa fix this car

(117) (a) *How many hours did John needa fix his car
     (b) *The three hours which we needa fix this car can't be found
     (c) *Take as much time as these cars needa be fixed

(118) (a) These weapons would be too big for us to want _____ to be shipped express
     (b) *These weapons would be too big for us to wanna be shipped express ($\neq$ (118a))

While allowing that the examples in (116b) and (117) do not "argue against Lightfoot's hypothesis if one takes comparatives to be formed by a movement rule," Emonds considers it "difficult to establish that a movement rule gives rise to the deletion site in [(118a)]" (1977, p. 242). For reasons given in Chapter 3, however, I find the *wh*-Movement analysis of examples such as (118a) to be convincing. Therefore I take (118b) as an example that confirms my own contention that *wh*-traces block contraction, while NP-traces and PRO (which I identify) do not. I consider this theory to be considerably more simple and explicit than Emonds's characterization of Bresnan's view: "If the intervening ma-

terial in V _____ to is removed by a rule whose domain
includes at least the COMP of the lowest clause containing
V, that material is still present when *to*-Adjunction applies,
and hence blocks the rule" (Emonds, 1977, p. 243). I am not
convinced, however, that the examples in (117b) constitute
pure instances of contraction blocked by a *wh*-trace, since
it could also be maintained that the "to" of reduced result
and purpose clauses cannot contract, presumably for structural reasons. Consider, in this light, the ambiguity of
(119a), which is resolved in (119b).

(119) (a) I'm going to please Fred
       (b) I'm gonna please Fred

While (119a) can mean that I am going in order to please
Fred or that I will please Fred, (119b) has only the latter
meaning. It is possible that the complements in (117) have
the result or purpose clause structure which apparently pro-
hibits contraction independently. In any event, the traditional examples leave little doubt that *wh*-traces do prevent
contraction.

In summary, given the necessary caveat with respect to
identifying the result of *to*-Adjunction, I believe that
Emonds's examples (114) and (115) constitute convincing
instances of contraction over NP-trace.

I am less convinced by the example given in Bresnan
(1978). Bresnan cites example (120a) with the analysis given
in (120b).

(120) (a) There's gonna be a movie made about us
       (b) There is going [_____ to be a movie made about us]

However, Bresnan denies the analysis in (120b) and considers the possibility of contraction in (120a) to constitute
part of an argument against the existence of a subject raising
transformation. Yet there is nothing "unexpected" about
this example if trace and PRO are identified and *wh*-traces
are held to block contraction. Whether there are such rules
as subject raising seems to be independent of the grammaticality of (120a). Bresnan suggests that "want" and "be
going" are "very much like modal verbs" and take infinitival

complements. Note, however, the following contrast:

(121) (a) John might wanna do it
      (b) *John might be gonna do it
           (Cf.: John might be going to do it)

It would seem impossible to analyze "wanna" as a modal in (121a) (since modals do not cooccur), while in (121b) "be gonna" apparently must be analyzed as a main verb, which status it apparently resists. It is perhaps best to claim that "be gonna" has modal status, not "be going." In any event, if this option is taken, (119b) would not constitute a case of contraction across an NP-trace.

I wish now to present an argument that contrasts contraction possibilities across NP-trace and *wh*-trace. It has the merit of contrasting the two types of trace in essentially the same positions. In order to present the relevant data, I must first consider the data in (122):

(122) (a) *I gave him it
      (b) *I gave John it
      (c)   I gave him a book

We may state the generalization as being that a structure containing a pronoun dominated by NP, which is not contracted onto the $[+V]$ element, is ungrammatical. We can propose that the rule of contraction applies only once, adjoining a pronoun to the $[+V]$ element to its immediate left. (122c) will be allowed, since "him" can adjoin, and the other examples will be ruled out by the suggested principle. An example such as (123) demonstrates (apparently correctly) that "gimme" is a lexical item.

(123) Gimme it

The generalization that a pronoun in a VP cannot be a free morpheme (in Standard American English) must be stated after NP-Movement, as (124) shows:

(124) He$_i$ was given e$_i$ it

This is as would be expected, since the generalization is a morphological one and should be stated at the level of surface structure, or at PR, the level that is the output of Hop C.

However, given the proposed generalization, (124) demonstrates something else, namely, that contraction can apply across an NP-trace. Contrast now the example in (125) with (124):

> (125) *Who$_i$ did John give e$_i$ it
> (Cf.: ?Who$_i$ did John give e$_i$ the book)

Apparently contraction is blocked in (125); but this is precisely as predicted if *wh*-traces block contraction. I consider the contrast between (124) and (125) to constitute another piece of evidence in favor of my proposal: NP-trace and PRO are identical and do not block contraction, while *wh*-trace does.[22]

THE SPECIFICITY CONDITION—ITS INTERACTION WITH EXTRAPOSITION

The specificity of an NP is, apparently, a parameter relevant to at least some of the relations of anaphora holding across NP-brackets.[23] The (b) cases below are inferior in grammaticality to the (a) examples:

> (126) (a) He$_i$ believes [$_{NP}$ pictures of himself$_i$]
>
>   to be on sale
>
>   (b) *He$_i$ believes [$_{NP}$ the picture of himself$_i$]
>
>   to be on sale
>
> (127) (a) The men$_i$ believe [$_{NP}$ pictures of each other$_i$]
>
>   to be on sale
>
>   (b) *The men$_i$ believe [$_{NP}$ those pictures of each other$_i$]
>
>   to be on sale

We will, for the moment, rely on a rough definition of specificity, which will include, for example, those NPs that contain initial possessives, and singular definite descriptions. As will be seen, the specificity notion is a complex one and may well constitute the interweaving of many different parameters, admit of degrees, and so forth. Some of these issues will be discussed in Chapter 5.

If these judgments are assumed, the following generalization would hold:

(128) *. . . X_i . . . $[_{NP}$ . . . X_i . . .] . . .

where NP is [+Specific]

It seems clear that Extraposition from NP is possible even if the NP extracted from is [+Specific]:

(129) (a) $[_{NP}$ That man e_i] came in $[_{S_i}$ that we talked about]

(b) $[_{NP}$ The fact e_i] remains $[_{S_i}$ that we lost]

The grammaticality of the examples in (129), under the analysis given, would seem to indicate that (128) cannot be generalized to (130):

(130) *. . . X_i . . . $[_{NP}$ . . . X_i . . .] . . . X_i . . .

where NP is [+Specific]

Yet data from PP-Extraposition seem to require that the Specificity Condition constrain the output of rightward movement:

(131) (a) *$[_{NP}$ The review e_i] came out yesterday

$[_i$of John's book]

(b) *$[_{NP}$ that review e_i] came out yesterday

$[_i$of John's book]

(Cf.: $[_{NP}$ A review e_i] came out yesterday

$[_i$of John's book])

It might appear that the problem posed by the contrast in grammaticality between the examples in (129) and (131) is that the Specificity Condition must be formulated so as to distinguish between the examples. An alternative, however, would be to propose that Extraposition from NP, unlike PP-Extraposition, relates to the levels of SS and PR, not DS and SS. Then, if the Specificity Condition is formulated as a condition on LF, the counterexamples to the Specificity Condition in (129) would be only apparent. The following diagram shows the positions of application of the relevant rules:

(132)

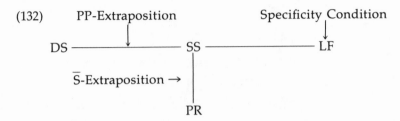

We will see below, however, that this proposal is untenable, and a more principled account is available.

It is of interest to note that one alternative proposal to that sketched in (132) is ruled out by independent considerations. Suppose that one formulated the Specificity Condition as follows:

(133) $*. \ldots X_i \ldots [_{\overline{\overline{N}}} \text{ SPEC } [_{\overline{N}} \ldots X_i \ldots]] \ldots X_i \ldots$

where $\overline{\overline{N}}$ is [+Specific]

If it were assumed, or independently argued, that the examples in (129) have the structure (134), as seems plausible, (133) would, correctly, not be applicable to (129), and the ordering of S-Extraposition as a rule relating SS and PR would be superfluous.

(134) $\ldots [_{\overline{\overline{N}}} \overline{\overline{N}} e_i] \ldots S_i \ldots$

This line of approach is probably precluded, however, by the fact that there is independent evidence, not based on S̄-Extraposition, which indicates that relative clause structures must, in fact, be distinguished by the Specificity Condition. The relevant examples are the following, cited in May (1977b) and Chomsky (1977e):[24]

(135) (a) We can't find books that have any missing pages
      (b) *We can't find the books that have any missing pages
      (c) *We can't find certain books that have any missing pages

What (135) suggests, then, is that the Specificity Condition should be formulated as applying to relative clause structures that are specific; (133), therefore, is not sufficiently general to capture the generalization.

By distinguishing PP-Extraposition and Extraposition from NP in such a way, it would be entailed that $\bar{S}$s extraposed from NP will behave as islands, while extraposed PPs need not do so. The examples in (136) illustrate the contrast:

(136) (a) *Who$_i$ did [$_{NP}$ the fact e$_j$] amaze Fred

[$_{\bar{S}_j}$ that Max saw e$_i$]

(b) Which book$_i$ has [$_{NP}$ a review e$_j$] come out

[$_{PP_j}$ of e$_i$]

Since $\bar{S}$-Extraposition will necessarily "follow" *wh*-Movement under the proposed theory, the structure to which *wh*-Movement applies will be "[$_{NP}$ the fact that Max saw who] amazed Fred," a violation of the NP Filter at SS and of the Specificity Condition at LF, as will be discussed in Chapter 5.

Let us now consider the possibility that PP-Extraposition and the Readjustment Rule are identical. To begin, it is clear that, given that the NP Filter applies at SS, the Readjustment Rule must apply before SS. Only on that assumption will structure (137) be allowed.

(137) Who$_j$ did John see [$_{NP}$ a picture e$_i$][$_{PP_i}$ of e$_j$]

Therefore, if PP-Extraposition and the Readjustment Rule are to be identical, all applications must apply before SS.

It is crucial now to point out that the Specificity Condition, which, as we will see, must apply at LF, is sensitive to Readjustment Rule outputs. Examples such as those in (139) are ruled out since the only possible sources that do not violate the NP Filter, those in (138), are themselves ruled out by the Specificity Condition, which is, necessarily, sensitive to rightward movement. This analysis is essentially that presented by Chomsky (1977e).

(138) (a) John saw [$_{NP}$ the picture e_i][$_{PP_i}$ of who]

(b) John saw [$_{NP}$ Bill's picture e_i][$_{PP_i}$ of who]

(139) (a) *Who did John see the picture of
(b) *Who did John see Bill's picture of

The question to ask, therefore, is whether the Specificity Condition is sensitive to PP-Extraposition outputs; relevant data were presented in (131). The ungrammaticality of these examples shows that there is no bar to identifying the two rules insofar as the Specificity Condition is concerned.

If the Readjustment Rule and PP-Extraposition are to be identified, the prediction would be that, in general, extraction is possible from extraposed PPs. I believe this to be the case. However, in the exhaustive study of PP-Extraposition by Guéron (1978), the conclusion is stated that an extraposed PP cannot be extracted from. The following data are presented:

(140) (a) A book came out by Chomsky
(b) ??Who did a book come out by

(141) (a) A man appeared with green eyes
(b) *What color eyes did a man appear with

Guéron notes that (140b) is better than (141b). She attributes this difference to the same constraint which explains the difference between the following examples:

(142) (a) Who did you read a book about
(b) *What color eyes did you meet a man with

It is, parenthetically, consistent with the view that the Readjustment Rule and PP-Extraposition are identical that both (141b) and (142b) are ungrammatical; the question is *why* they are ungrammatical.

Note that (143) is grammatical, but (144) is not:

(143) Nosferatu appeared (to him) with green eyes

(144) *What color eyes did Nosferatu appear (to him) with

And, of course, (145) is also ungrammatical.

(145) *Nosferatu with green eyes appeared (to him)

I conclude that whatever blocks the extraction in (144), it cannot depend on PP-Extraposition, since (143) clearly cannot derive from (145). Therefore, the ungrammaticality of (142b) does not count against the claim that extraposed PPs allow extraction.

There are, furthermore, other grammatical instances of extraction from extraposed PPs:

(146) (a) Discussions have occurred about several topics
      (b) Which topics have discussions occurred about

(147) (a) Congratulations have arrived from the usual sycophants
      (b) Which sycophants have congratulations arrived from

(148) (a) Explanations have never appeared for those sightings
      (b) Which sightings have explanations never appeared for

The contrast between the (b) examples of (146) through (148) with the examples in (149) is exactly as the NP Filter would predict, of course:

(149) (a) *Which topics have discussions about occurred
      (b) *Which sycophants have congratulations from arrived
      (c) *Which sightings have explanations for never appeared

A few initial conclusions may be stated with respect to the Specificity Condition. It appears, first of all, that the Specificity Condition is sensitive to the outputs of the PP-Extraposition/Readjustment Rule. The ordering of the Specificity Condition might, from the point of view of the data stated here, be either at SS or LF.

Let us now return to the status of Extraposition from NP. There are further data relevant to deciding which component the PP-Extraposition/Readjustment Rule and Extraposition from NP apply in.

Consider first the following contrasts, in which underlining indicates intended coreference:

(150) (a) I gave [a book about <u>Nixon</u>] to <u>him</u>
      (b) *I gave [a book e_i] to <u>him</u> [$_{PP_i}$ about Nixon][25]

(151) (a)   I sent [a painting by <u>Picasso</u>] to <u>him</u>

(b)   *I sent [a painting e_i] to <u>him</u> [$_{PP_i}$ by <u>Picasso</u>]

These data are as expected, given that PP-Extraposition precedes SS, the level that is input to the mechanisms that determine possibilities of reference. They pattern with the data of *it*-Extraposition, in fact, and we infer that both (152a) and (152b) must appear at SS as well:

(152) (a)   That <u>Nixon</u> had been challenged irritated <u>him</u>

(b)   *It irritated <u>him</u> that <u>Nixon</u> had been challenged

The possibilities of reference in Extraposition from NP sentences are the same as those considered in the previous two paradigms:

(153) (a)   They proposed [the idea that <u>Fred</u> should resign] to <u>him</u>

(b)   *They proposed [the idea e_i] to <u>him</u> [$_{S_i}$ that <u>Fred</u>

should resign]

Since we assume that SS constitutes the input to the mechanisms determining possibilities of reference, we conclude that both (153a) and (153b) must be present at SS.

There was, the reader will recall, a desirable consequence of placing Extraposition from NP in the component relating SS and PR; this was that the ungrammaticality of (154a) and (b) would follow from the NP Filter, assuming that that filter applies at SS.

(154) (a)   *Who$_i$ did [the fact [that Max hated e_i]] amaze Bill

(b)   *Who$_i$ did [the fact e_j] amaze Bill [$_{S_j}$ that Max hated e_i]

We must, therefore, find an alternative explanation for the ungrammaticality of (at least) (154b).

We may approach a solution by expanding the problem. We begin with the following contrast:

(155) (a)   It wasn't obvious that he had any talent

(b)   *The fact wasn't obvious that he had any talent

If Extraposition from NP applied "after" SS, the ungrammaticality of (155b) would follow from the ungrammaticality of (156), whatever its source:

(156) *The fact that he had any talent wasn't obvious

We note, however, that the data do not divide in such a way that all *it*-Extraposition sentences parallel to (155a) are grammatical.

Consider the following:

(157) (a) *It didn't bother you that John had any talent
    (b) *It wasn't odd that John had any talent
    (c) *It wasn't remembered that John had any talent

We notice a familiar class of predicates in these examples: the "factives" of Kiparsky and Kiparksy (1970). And we notice the further characteristic fact that the factive complements resist extraction:

(158) (a) *Who did it bother you that Max hated
    (b) *Who was it odd that Karl noticed
    (c) *Who was it remembered that Joe purged

Suppose, then, that factive complements may contain no free variables at LF. The obligatory extraction of "any" in (155b) would now be filtered out by the same mechanism that blocks (157) and (158). We will end this speculation here, however, to return to it in Chapter 5, where the possible relationships of the Factivity Filter to the Specificity Condition will be examined.

Subjacency

In the section that follows, the term "subjacency filter" will refer to any filter of the general form (160):

$$(160) \quad *. \ . \ . \ X_i \ . \ . \ . \ [_\alpha \ . \ . \ . \ [_\beta \ . \ . \ . \ Y_i \ . \ . \ .$$

where α and β are "bounding nodes"

The question to be asked is whether, given the system of filters developed so far, there is any independent motivation for a subjacency filter.

It is obvious that if α and β in (160) are identified as NP, and the subjacency filter so defined is stipulated to apply at

SS, the filter would be superfluous, being merely a special case of the NP Filter. Therefore, in order to establish independent motivation for a subjacency filter at the level of SS, bounding nodes other than NP must be considered.

Consider S as a candidate:

(161) *. . . X_i . . . $[_S$ . . . $[_S$ . . . Y_i . . .

It is clear that (161) cannot be appealed to as a filter on *wh*-Movement outputs, since examples such as (162) are grammatical, given our assumptions:

(162) Who$_i$ $[_S$ do you believe that $[_S$ Max saw e$_i$]]

Overgeneration by *wh*-Movement is reduced by the NP and Priority Filters—the first incorporating most of the classical "island" phenomena of Ross (1967), the second the "*wh*-island condition."

With respect to NP-Movement outputs, it appears that (161) is totally subsumed by the Priority Filter. Consider first an example such as (163):

(163) *John$_i$ believes $[_S$ Fred$_j$ to be known $[_S$ e$_i$ to be crazy]]

(163) violates the Priority Filter; however, (164) does not.

(164) *John$_i$ wants $[_S$ e$_i$ to know $[_S$ e$_i$ to be crazy]]

(164) contrasts with (165):

(165) John$_i$ is believed $[_S$ e$_i$ to have been known

$[_S$ e$_i$ to be crazy]]

Given the grammaticality of (165), it is clear that (161) cannot be appealed to block (164). It is equally clear that the ungrammaticality of (164) derives from the ill-formedness of (166a), as against (166b); lexical properties relevant to the control relation are responsible.

(166) (a) *John$_i$ knew $[_S$ e$_i$ to be crazy]

(b) John$_i$ was known $[_S$ e$_i$ to be crazy]

Clearly subjacency is irrelevant to this contrast. Given the independent necessity of such a theory of control, it seems that (161) is superfluous with respect to NP-Movement.

A completely parallel demonstration could be made with respect to the putative bounding node $\bar{S}$—in fact, it already has been, in effect, in connection with examples (164) and (165).

It appears, therefore, that given the NP Filter, there is no necessity for the Subjacency Filter to constrain outputs of NP-Movement and *wh*-Movement. Subjacency may play a role with regard to PP and $\bar{S}$-Extraposition, but this remains problematical, due to the possibility of successive cyclic application (see Akmajian, 1975, note 4). We must now turn to the major task of this chapter, however, which is to draw certain metatheoretical conclusions from the filters developed so far.

Conclusion

In this chapter we have posited three filters, the NP Filter and the Priority Filter, which apply at SS and PR, respectively, and the Specificity Condition, which applies at LF. This last filter will be investigated in more detail in the following chapter. The Priority Filter has been given independent motivation in Chapter 2.

It is my belief that the Priority Filter subsumes the "*wh*-Island Condition" as well as the Superiority Condition, insofar as this last is accurate. This filter also subsumes certain violations of the Specified Subject Condition which involve $[_{NP}\ e]$, though redundantly, as has been pointed out.

It is also my belief that the Subjacency Condition would be superfluous in the theory constructed here. Since the Subjacency Condition has been taken to be the diagnostic property of certain movement rules, dispensing with this condition calls into question the existence of these rules. The rules I am referring to are, of course, NP-Movement and *wh*-Movement.

The issue as to whether *wh*-Movement and NP-Movement should be recast as rules of construal is a complex one. Consider a grammar that contains not only *wh*-Movement and NP-Movement but also a rule that coindexes *e* with another NP (for example, control of PRO). If the conditions on the application of movement and coindexing are different, either by reason of explicit stipulation within particular grammars or by reason of metatheoretical considerations, the desirability of postulating that there is just one type of rule (coindexing, say) would be reduced. If the conditions on the application of the movement rules and the coindexing rule are the same (and this would include as an ideal case the situation in which there are *no* conditions on their application, either grammar-specific or universal), then the desirability of postulating that there is just one type of rule would rest on whether the system of filters that constrains the output of a very general coindexing mechanism would have to be made more complex in order to subsume both the "movement data" and the "coindex data." If one holds, with Chomsky (1977e), that the Subjacency Condition constrains the application of movement rules, the first kind of difficulty is faced. If this assumption is dropped, however, and the effects previously explained by postulating sub⌐ jacency are explained by independently necessary mechanisms, as is proposed in this chapter, the question is then whether the filters that view the outputs of a very general rule of coindexing induce a corresponding bifurcation in rule types. Although these considerations are not the only ones involved in such a choice, they are central to it, or at least so it seems to me. Note that the issue is *not* whether or not there are movement rules; it would in fact be crucial in a theory that dropped *wh*-Movement and NP-Movement in favor of a coindexing mechanism applying to base-generated "traces" that there be movement rules (for example, the QR of May (1977a)) in the derivation relating SS and LF. The issue, rather, centers on questions such as whether one system of filters can appropriately constrain the positions of PRO and trace, the *e* elements, indiscriminately. I believe that I have, indeed, constructed such a system.

I do not, however, consider this result to be particularly significant. The choice between a very general movement rule and a very general coindexing rule seems to have little empirical impact. Since PRO could as easily be an element that is assigned its index via movement as by a rule of construal in this framework, the question as to whether there is movement becomes a question as to how indices are assigned. While empirically significant arguments can be imagined which would decide such a issue, they appear to me to be at a level of metatheoretical abstraction which can hardly be approached with confidence, given the current state of the art. Thus I leave this question open, hoping only that it has been well defined.

Of much greater significance, in my opinion, is the question of modularity and the question of the level of application of the various filters. These issues have direct empirical consequences and determine the nature of the idealization of the form of grammar itself. In the chapter that follows, these issues will be pursued, focusing on the level of LF.

5

Topics in the Syntax
of Logical Form

In this chapter I wish to present some speculations concerning membership at the level of LF. While theorizing is speculative by its very nature, it is particularly so in this case, since the properties of LF have only recently received any detailed attention. I will rely largely on the pioneering work of Chomsky (1978) as well as that of May (1977a), Higginbotham (in press), and Higginbotham and May (1979a, 1979b, in press), some of whose findings will be outlined below.

I assume that at the level of LF, intuitions are represented concerning the quantificational and anaphoric properties of the sentences of a language. I rely on the proposal of May (1977) that there exists a rule, Quantifier Raising (QR), which Chomsky-adjoins quantifiers to S, thereby giving them their scopes, the traces of the quantifiers being interpreted as the variables which they bind. This rule is a movement rule relating SS and LF. Filters at LF, one of which, the Specificity Condition, will be mentioned below, determine the possible scopes that a quantifier might have in a particular sentence, as well as determining those scopes that a quantifier may not have. The goals pursued in the construction of LF are internal to linguistic theory; I assume that the construction of this level is an empirical matter, parallel in this respect to the construction of other levels of representation in grammar. The construction of an appropriate semantics for this linguistic level has received little attention as of this writing, but I refer the reader to Higginbotham (forthcoming) which contains, among other things, some valuable insights concerning the semantics of questions. As a last point of clarification, I wish to emphasize that the term "LF" is not to be confused with the term "logical form" as it is used in the domain of pure logic or mathematics; the representations of intuitions concerning the logical properties of natural language need not be precisely equivalent to logical representations constructed in other formal systems for other purposes.

Some Assumptions Concerning LF

Indexing and Opacity

In this section I will present a brief summary of the Indexing Algorithm and related mechanisms presented in Chomsky (1978). It is in the context of this theoretical advance that the notions sketched in this chapter are presented.

The first sort of case to consider is that of movement. In accordance with "Trace Theory," we may say that the rule "Move α" converts a labeled bracketing of the form (1) into a labeled bracketing of the form (2a) or (2b):

(1) $\ldots [_\alpha X] \ldots$

(2) (a) $\ldots [_{\alpha_i} X] \ldots [_{\alpha_i} e] \ldots$

    (b) $\ldots [_{\alpha_i} e] \ldots [_{\alpha_i} X] \ldots$

The index i will be an index previously unused in the derivation, by convention; if α is already indexed by a previous movement rule as α_j, then, by convention, we may let $i = j$. This yields a partial indexing in surface structure.

Taking these partially indexed structures, further indices

are assigned to the remaining NPs; indices are assigned to the full sentence from top to bottom, an NP being indexed only when all NPs that c-command it or dominate it have been indexed.

Further indexing is assigned by "rules of construal"; PRO,[1] the reflexive, and the reciprocal are coindexed with antecedents. The items indexed by rules of construal are termed "anaphors."

Indices assigned by the three previous mechanisms may be termed "referential indices."

We may now assign to each non-anaphor an "anaphoric index," which is the set containing the referential index of each NP that c-commands the non-anaphor. In the example given in (3), the first index of each NP is its referential index; the set that follows is its anaphoric index.

(3) $[_{NP_2}$ John] told $[_{NP_{(3,(2))}}$ Bill] about $[_{NP_{(4,(2,3))}}$ him]

I follow Higginbotham (in press) in assuming that this Indexing Algorithm applies before QR.

The anaphoric index of an NP α is interpreted as stating that α is disjoint in reference from each NP whose referential index appears in the anaphoric index of α. This corresponds to intuition in examples such as (3).

We may now turn to the "binding conditions," which delete indices of anaphors and pronouns under specified conditions.

Consider first examples such as (4a) and (4b):

(4) (a) John expected him to win
    (b) John expected he would win

The Indexing Algorithm will yield (5a) and (5b), respectively:

(5) (a) $[_{NP_2}$ John] expected $[_{NP_{(3,(2))}}$ him] to win

    (b) $[_{NP_2}$ John] expected $[_{NP_{(3,(2))}}$ he] would win

The interpretation of anaphoric indices suggested yields the correct result in (5a), though not in (5b). Furthermore, (6) has the predicted interpretation:

(6) (a) $[_{NP_2}$ John] expected $[_{NP_{(3,(2))}}$ Bill] $\begin{Bmatrix} to \\ would \end{Bmatrix}$ win

Delaying discussion of (5b), consider (7a) and (7b):

(7) (a) $[_{NP_2}$ John] expected $[_{NP_2}$ himself] to win

(b) *$[_{NP_2}$ John] expected $[_{NP_2}$ himself] would win

Chomsky unifies discussion of examples such as (5b) and (7b) by appealing to the notion "designated index." A designated index of an NP α is its anaphoric index, if it has one; otherwise the referential index of α is its designated index.

Given this notion, we may now present Chomsky's definition of the notion "free":[2]

(8) Suppose that α has the designated index j and i is an integer such that $i = j$ or $i \in j$. Then α is *free(i)* in β if there is no γ in β with index i that c-commands α.

We may now state the Nominative Island Condition (NIC):[3]

(9) Suppose that α has the designated index j and is free(i) in β (β = NP or S) where (a) α is nominative. Then $j \to 0$ if j is an integer, and $j \to (j - \{i\})$ if j is a set.

The NIC will apply to (5b) to yield (10) and (7b) to yield (11):

(10) $[_{NP_2}$ John] expected $[_{NP_3}$ he] would win

(11) $[_{NP_2}$ John] expected $[_{NP_0}$ himself] would win

We now have the desired result, given the binding condition in (9), if it is stipulated that NP_0 is not permitted at LF, where 0 is a referential index.

We may conclude this brief summary of the theory presented in Chomsky (1978) by considering structure (12):

(12) $[_{NP_2}$ John] wanted $[_{NP_{(3,(2))}}$ Bill] to visit $[_{NP_{(4,(2,3))}}$ him]

As represented, (12) is contrary to intuition, since "John" and "him" may corefer in such structures. Consequently, we must add the condition to (9) given in (13):

(13) or (b) α is in the domain of the subject of β, β minimal[4]

With this condition, 3 in the anaphoric index of "him" deletes, as desired. Were a reflexive in the position of "him" and coindexed with "John," its referential index would delete, leading to the prevented referential index 0, as in (11).

We also assume a rule Quantifier Raising (QR), which adjoins Qs to S, giving them their scope, as discussed in May (1977a). Given a structure as in (14a), (14b) is produced.

(14) (a) $[_S$ John loves $[_{NP_i}$ everyone$]]$

    (b) $[_S[_{NP_i}$ everyone$][_S$ John loves $e_i]]$

I assume that this rule applies to *wh*-words as well as elements that are more traditionally assumed to be quantifiers. QR relates SS and LF, and follows the Indexing Algorithm.

Variables and Traces at LF

In this section I will consider the implications of a proposal, due originally, I believe, to Chomsky, that at the level of LF, variables are to be identified with traces which are assigned Case. As will be seen, this proposed identification yields a quite natural theory of the position of variables in structures that contain more than one trace. Furthermore, when coupled with the Indexing Algorithm described in the preceding section, this hypothesis is sufficient to explain why certain applications of "Move NP" and "Move *wh*" yield ungrammatical structures. The theory of variable position presented thus serves as a filtering device much like the other mechanisms in previous chapters.

As an initial illustrative example, consider the derivations of (15):

(15) Who was hit

Example (15) has an SS as in (16):

(16) Who_2 $[e_2$ was hit $e_2]$

Structure (16) derives by an application of "Move NP," which fronts "who_2" to subject position, followed by an application of "Move *wh*."

Consider now the problem of determining the correct position of the variable in the LF of (16). In principle, any of the structures of (17) would be available if traces were interpreted as variables optionally:

(17) (a) who $_{x_2: x_2 \text{ a person}}$ [e$_2$ was hit e$_2$]

    (b) who $_{x_2: x_2 \text{ a person}}$ [x$_2$ was hit e$_2$]

    (c) who $_{x_2: x_2 \text{ a person}}$ [e$_2$ was hit x$_2$]

    (d) who $_{x_2: x_2 \text{ a person}}$ [x$_2$ was hit x$_2$]

Three of the structures in (17) are clearly inappropriate, however. Structure (17a) is not well formed since it contains no variable for the quantifier to bind.[5] Structure (17d) is inappropriate, since it wrongly represents the predicate "was hit" as reflexive. Note that if traces were *identified with* variables, as was done, for example, in Fiengo (1974), *only* (17d) would be generated at LF, an incorrect result. Of (17b) and (17c), only (17b) seems appropriate, for reasons that will be given shortly.

Consider the structure of (16) in more detail. After the assignment of Case, we will have the structure (18):

(18) $[_{\text{SPEC}}[_{\text{NP}_2}$ who$]][_{\text{NP}_2}$ e] was hit $[_{\text{NP}_2}$ e]]
      [−Obl]   [−Obl]

Since "hit" in (18) is analyzed as an adjective, it of course does not assign Case to the trace that follows it. The trace in subject position in (18) does receive Case, however, and there are at least two ways in which Case assignment might be effected in this structure. On the one hand, a theory might be constructed in which Case assignment precedes the movement of the *wh*-word into SPEC. On this view, (19) would immediately underlie (18).

(19) $[_{\text{SPEC}}$ e$][[_{\text{NP}_2}$ who] was hit $[_{\text{NP}_2}$ e]]
         [−Obl]

Assuming that the Case feature [−Obl] (which is realized as Nominative in Ss) belongs to the set of nonterminal features, it will, of course, be "left behind" in (18), as are the feature specifications of NP and the referential index. On the other hand, one might assume that Case assignment follows "Move *wh*." If this theory is to be adequate, it must be coupled with a convention to the effect that if an NP dominating *e* is assigned Case *c*, then Case *c* must also be assigned to the NP that binds *e*. I mention these options but will not attempt to discriminate between them here (but see Chapter 2).

Notice now that if variables are identified with Cased traces at the level of LF, we have the result that corresponding to the SS (18) we will have the LF (17b).

In contrast to the derivation of "who was hit," consider the derivation of the ungrammatical example (20):

(20) *Who hit

Example (20) might have (21) as a deep structure:

(21) $[_{SPEC} e][[_{NP_2} e]$ hit $[_{NP_3}$ who]]

After "Move NP" and "Move *wh*" we will have (22):

(22) $[_{SPEC}[_{NP_3}$ who]$[[_{NP_3} e]$ hit $[_{NP_3} e]]$

Case assignment produces (23):

(23) $[_{SPEC}[_{NP_3}$ who]$[[_{NP_3} e]$ hit $[_{NP_3} e]]$
$\quad$ [−Obl] $\quad$ [−Obl] $\quad$ [+Obl]

If all Cased traces are variables, we will have LF (24) corresponding to SS (23).

(24) who $_{x_3: x_3 \text{ a person}}$ $[x_3 \text{ hit } x_3]$

Structure (24) is well formed as represented. It would naturally be interpreted in the same way as the LF of (25) is:

(25) Who hit himself

Consequently, we lack an explanation for the ungrammaticality of (20).

In order to construct such an explanation, let us alter the assumptions of the "On Binding" framework in such a way that anaphoric indices are assigned to Cased traces. If Case assignment follows "Move *wh*," we must of course require that the referential index of the *wh*-word moved by *wh*-Movement not appear in the anaphoric index of its trace. If this is not prevented, (27) would automatically derive from (26):

(26) $[_{SPEC}[_{NP_2}$ who$]][_S[_{NP_2}$ e] left]
    $\phantom{[_{SPEC}}[-Obl][-Obl]$

(27) $[_{SPEC}[_{NP_2}$ who$]][_S[_{NP_{(2,\{2\})}}$ e] left]
    $\phantom{[_{SPEC}}[-Obl][-Obl]$

This restriction is a perfectly reasonable one; since "who" is to be interpreted as a quantifier, we may state that only NPs in argument position "donate" their referential indices to the anaphoric indices of other NPs.

Assuming, then, that Cased traces are assigned anaphoric indices (and that a quantifier cannot donate its referential index to the anaphoric index of an NP), we may return to the derivation of *"who hit."

Structure (24) will now be replaced by the more detailed (28), given our assumptions:

(28) who $_{x_3:\ x_3\ a\ person}$ $[[_{NP_3}$ e] hit $[_{NP_{(3,\{3\})}}$ e]]
    $\phantom{(28)\ who\ _{x_3:\ x_3\ a\ person}\ [[_{NP_3}}[-Obl]\phantom{\ e]\ hit\ [_{NP_{(3,\{3\})}}}[+Obl]$

But (28) is ruled out, due to the presence of the contradictory index in the NP in object position. Consequently, we have an explanation for the ungrammaticality of *"who hit."

Note that we have as an entailment the observation that (25) cannot have an LF as in (28), suggesting that (29) is the appropriate LF structure:

(29) who $_{x_3:\ x_3\ a\ person}$ $[[_{NP_3}$ e] hit $[_{NP_3}$ himself]]
    $\phantom{(29)\ who\ _{x_3:\ x_3\ a\ person}\ [[_{NP_3}}[-Obl]\phantom{\ e]\ hit\ [_{NP_3}}[+Obl]$

Since, as mentioned above, the reflexive does not receive an anaphoric index, the possibility of a contradictory index does not arise. By treating the reflexive (as well as the reciprocal) as a constant and not as a variable at LF, we assign to the rules interpreting LF the task of providing interpretations for these notions.[6] It is suggestive to note, then, that the reflexive relation is inherent in certain lexical items ("self-pity," and so forth) and that the reciprocal relation seems to be contained in such words as "converse." It seems, therefore, that positioning the rules interpreting the reflexive and the reciprocal in the SR-2 component, which relates LF and SR, may be the correct idealization, since this is the component that independently provides the interpretations of these lexical items.

Returning to the interaction of Case and variable position, we note that we have a straightforward account of why (30) is impossible:

(30) *Who was Bill hit

Example (30) would have an SS as in (31):

(31) $[_{SPEC}[_{NP_3}$ who]][$[_{NP_2}$ Bill] was hit $[_{NP_3}$ e]]
$[-Obl]$

Since the NP following "hit" is not assigned Case, "hit" being an adjective, there is no variable at LF which the quantifier can bind. Consequently, (30) is ruled out at the level of LF. Example (31) is also ruled out, it should be mentioned, by the requirement that all lexical NPs must be assigned Case.[7] Since "who" in (31) cannot inherit Case from the position which it binds, and cannot be assigned Case in the position in which it stands, (31) is also ruled out on this account. This requirement appears to be independently necessary in order to rule out (32):

(32) *John was hit Fred

The derivation of the ungrammatical *"who was seen Bill by" illustrates both a violation of the requirement that lexical NP have Case as well as an instance of a contradictory index. Given a deep structure as in (33), (34) will be derived by "Move NP" and (35) by "Move *wh.*"

(33) $[_{SPEC}$ e]][$[_{NP_2}$ who] was seen $[_{NP_3}$ Bill] by $[_{NP_4}$ e]]

(34) $[_{\text{SPEC}}$ e$][[_{\text{NP}_2}$ e] was seen $[_{\text{NP}_3}$ Bill] by $[_{\text{NP}_2}$ who]]

(35) $[_{\text{SPEC}}[_{\text{NP}_2}$ who]][$[_{\text{NP}_2}$ e] was seen $[_{\text{NP}_3}$ Bill] by $[_{\text{NP}_2}$ e]]

Case assignment produces (36):

$$(36)\ [_{\text{SPEC}}[_{\text{NP}_2}\ \text{who}]][[_{\text{NP}_2}\ \text{e}]\ \text{was seen}$$
$$[-\text{Obl}] \qquad\qquad [-\text{Obl}]$$
$$[_{\text{NP}_2}\ \text{Bill}]\ \text{by}\ [_{\text{NP}_2}\ \text{e}]]$$
$$[+\text{Obl}]$$

And the Indexing Algorithm yields (37):

$$(37)\ [_{\text{SPEC}}[_{\text{NP}_2}\ \text{who}]][[_{\text{NP}_2}\ \text{e}]\ \text{was seen}$$
$$[-\text{Obl}] \qquad\qquad [-\text{Obl}]$$
$$[_{\text{NP}_3}\ \text{Bill}]\ \text{by}\ [_{\text{NP}_{(2,\{2\})}}\ \text{e}]]$$
$$[+\text{Obl}]$$

Structure (37) contains two violations; "Bill" lacks Case, and the final trace bears a contradictory index.

The NIC and Traces at LF

The theory outlined here has some implications for the formulation of the NIC. Consider first the examples in (38):

(38) (a) *John believes is crazy
    (b) *John believes himself is crazy
    (c) *The men believe each other are crazy

Under the assumptions of the "On Binding" framework, the examples of (38) all fall under the NIC. The NIC applies to the structures in (39) to yield (40):

(39) (a) $[_{\text{NP}_2}$ John] believes $[_{\text{NP}_2}$ e] is crazy

    (b) $[_{\text{NP}_2}$ John] believes $[_{\text{NP}_2}$ himself] is crazy

    (c) $[_{\text{NP}_2}$ the men] believe $[_{\text{NP}_2}$ each other] are crazy

(40) (a) $[_{\text{NP}_2}$ John] believes $[_{\text{NP}_0}$ e] is crazy

    (b) $[_{\text{NP}_2}$ John] believes $[_{\text{NP}_0}$ himself] is crazy

(c) $[_{NP_2}$ John] believes $[_{NP_0}$ each other] is crazy

The prohibition that NP_0 is not allowed at LF serves to rule out the structures in (40).

Given the proposal advanced here, in which Cased traces are assigned anaphoric indices, the account of why (38a) is ungrammatical must be altered. Example (38a) will have an SS as in (41), not as in (39a).

(41) $[_{NP_2}$ John] believes $[_{NP_{(2,\{2\})}}$ e] is crazy
$\quad\;\;$ [−Obl] $\qquad\qquad\qquad$ [−Obl]

If no other rule applied to (41), we would have the desired result that (38a) is ungrammatical, since (41) contains a contradictory index. The NIC, however, applies to (41), deleting the anaphoric index of the trace. The unobjectionable structure (42) is produced:

(42) $[_{NP_2}$ John] believes $[_{NP_2}$ e] is crazy

The derivation just given is parallel, on this theory, to that given in (43):

(43) (a) $[_{NP_2}$ John] believes $[_{NP_{(3,\{2\})}}$ he] is crazy

$\quad\;\;$ (b) $[_{NP_2}$ John] believes $[_{NP_3}$ he] is crazy

In order to avoid this consequence, we simply deny that traces undergo the NIC and Opacity. We will, therefore, be left with the LF (41) corresponding to (38a), the desired result. On this account, trace and lexical elements such as "Bill" behave identically with respect to the operation of the NIC and Opacity: they do not undergo them. The NIC, of course, is prevented from applying to "Bill" in (44):

(44) $[_{NP_2}$ John] believes $[_{NP_{(3,\{2\})}}$ Bill] is crazy

The impossibility of "Move NP" following "Move *wh*" in a derivation, as illustrated in (45), now follows as a consequence.

(45) (a) $[_{NP_2}$ e] believes $[_{SPEC}$ e$][_{NP_3}$ Max] hit $[_{NP_4}$ who]

(b) $[_{NP_2}$ e] believes $[_{SPEC}[_{NP_4}$ who]]

$[_{NP_3}$ Max] hit $[_{NP_4}$ e]

(c) $[_{NP_4}$ who] believes $[_{SPEC}[_{NP_4}$ e]]

$[_{NP_3}$ Max] hit $[_{NP_4}$ e]

After the application of the Indexing Algorithm, the final trace will contain a contradictory index.[8] Since, again, trace does not undergo Opacity in this analysis, the anaphoric index of the final trace cannot delete.

On this analysis, then, (38a) is ruled out by the contradictory index filter, while (38b) and (38c) are ruled out by NIC.

Subjacency and Variables

The observations made in Chapters 3 and 4 concerning Subjacency are in no way affected by the proposals made here. Recall that by dropping Subjacency as a condition on application, we allow both derivations in which Subjacency is respected and *wh*-Movement is successive cyclic as well as derivations in which Subjacency is violated. In short, by dropping Subjacency as a condition of application, we allow *wh*-Movement to apply freely. Recall also that Subjacency cannot be appealed to if reformulated as a filter, given the theory of complementizer structure defended here. The insertion of complementizers will always cover traces of *wh*-Movement left in complementizer position, as illustrated in (46):

(46) (a) $[_{SPEC}[_{NP}$ · · ·]] · · · $[_{SPEC}[_{NP}$ e]] · · · $[_{NP}$ e]
$\qquad$ [wh] $\qquad\qquad$ [wh] $\qquad\qquad$ [wh]

(b) $[_{SPEC}[_{NP}$ · · ·]] · · · $[_{SPEC}$ that] · · · $[_{NP}$ e]
$\qquad$ [wh] $\qquad\qquad\qquad\qquad$ [wh]

Notice that the insertion of complementizers to cover these traces removes the possibility of interpreting these traces as variables, a welcome result.

Variables and Control

The analysis of variables presented here has interesting entailments for the treatment of PRO that was discussed in Chapter 4. Consider an example such as (47):

(47) John wants to leave

Assuming that *e* is coindexed at the level of SS, as suggested in Chapter 4, we will have an SS as in (48), before the application of the Indexing Algorithm:

(48) $[_{NP_2}$ John] wants $[[_{SPEC}$ e$][_{NP_2}$ e] to leave]]

The Indexing Algorithm must be prevented from producing (49):

(49) $[_{NP_2}$ John] wants $[[_{SPEC}$ e$][_{NP_{(2,(2))}}$ e] to leave]]

This result would be expected, given that Case must be assigned to "him" in (50):

(50) $[_{NP_2}$ John] wants $[[_{SPEC}$ e$][_{NP_{(3,(2))}}$ him] to leave]]

Furthermore, if variables are to be identified with Cased traces, Case must be assigned to the subject of the complement sentence in (51):

(51) $[_{NP_2}$ who] does John$_3$ want $[[_{SPEC}$ e]
[wh]
$[[_{NP_{(2,(3))}}$ e] to leave]]
[wh]

How is Case to be assigned in (50), and how are (49) and (51) to be distinguished?

Taking the second half of this question first, we recall that (49) and (51) are also to be distinguished with respect to contraction possibilities; "wanna" is a possible pronunciation of "want to" in (49) but not (51). It is possible to exploit this fact.

I propose that the rule of contraction apply in two steps, as follows:

(52) (a) $\ldots$ V $[_{SPEC}$ e$][_{NP}$ e] to $\ldots \rightarrow \ldots$ V to

$[_{SPEC}$ e$][_{NP}$ e] e $\ldots$,

where V is a member of {want, . . .}
(b) want to $\rightarrow$ wanna

The rule in (52a) is quite general, although there is a limitation to be discussed below, while (52b) is idiosyncratic, applying only to "want" and perhaps a few other verbs.

I assume that (52a) is a readjustment rule applying before SS, but that (52b) is a phonological rule. I also assume that a verb may assign Case to the subject of a complement sentence only if there is no terminal element unequal to e intervening. Lastly, I assume Case assignment is obligatory, as in all other circumstances.

Since the NP in (52a) lacks the [wh] specification, the rule moving "to" next to "want" will not be applicable to structure (51), as desired. If rule (52a) does not apply, (49) will be produced, but if it does, we will have (53):

(53) $[_{NP_2}$ John] wants to $[_{SPEC}$ e$][_{NP_2}$ e] e leave

Since "to" intervenes between the verb "wants" and the NP subject of the complement sentence (and "to" $\neq e$), Case will not be assigned to the NP and the i-set-i Filter will be avoided. The assignment of Case in (50) is without difficulty; "John wants to leave" is assigned structure (53), not (49), and (51) is correctly allowed, since (52a) is optional.
Consider now (54):

(54) *John was wanted to win

(54) will be assigned structure (55):

(55) $[_{NP_2}$ John] was wanted $[_{SPEC}$ e$][_{NP_2}$ e] to win
[-THAT]

Recall that in Chapter 2 it was noted that the non-$\emptyset$ allomorph of FOR must appear following adjectives, and that passive participles are analyzed as members of this category. Consequently, (55) is precluded and (56) is forced.

(56) *John was wanted for to win

But (56), if Prefixation applies, is precluded by AP, and if Prefixation does not apply, it is precluded by the stipulation that "for" is intrinsically bound. We have achieved a general account of the distribution of *e* subjects of the complement of "want."

We may now turn to "believe." Sentence (57) will be allowed, since "believe" does not select the FOR complementizer.[9]

(57) John was believed to be crazy

Both (58) and (59) will be allowed, since Case can be assigned.

(58) $[_{NP_2}$ John] believed $[_{SPEC}$ e$][_{NP_{(3,(2))}}$ him] to be crazy
$\phantom{(58) [_{NP_2} \text{John] believed } [_{SPEC} \text{e}]}$[+Obl]

(59) $[_{NP_2}$ Who] does $[_{NP_3}$ John] believe $[_{SPEC}$ e$][_{NP_{(2,(3))}}$ e]
$\phantom{(59) [_{NP_2} \text{Who] does } [_{NP_3} \text{John] believe } [_{SPEC} \text{e}]}$[+Obl]

   to be crazy

Example (60) may be blocked if "believe" does not belong to the set of verbs in (52a); the structure will be (61), not (62).

(60) *John believed to be crazy

(61) $[_{NP_2}$ John] believed $[_{SPEC}$ e$][_{NP_{(2,(2))}}$ e] to be crazy
$\phantom{(61) [_{NP_2} \text{John] believed } [_{SPEC} \text{e}]}$[+Obl]

(62) $[_{NP_2}$ John] believed to $[_{SPEC}$ e$][_{NP_2}$ e] be crazy

We are now prepared to consider the contrast between (63a) and (63b):

(63) (a) $[_i$Who] do you believe e_i left
     (b) *$[_{NP}$ The man $[_ie][_ie]$ left] was Fred

More explicitly, the SSs of (63a) and (63b) will be as in (64a) and (64b):

(64) (a) [$_{SPEC}$ [$_{NP}$ Who]] do you believe [$_{SPEC}$ e]
     [+WH] [wh]$_i$ [+THAT]
           [−Obl]   [−WH]

     [$_{NP}$ e] left
     [wh]$_i$
     [−Obl]

(b) [$_{NP}$[$_{NP}$ The man [$_{SPEC}$ [$_{NP}$ e]]
                    [+THAT] [wh]$_i$
                    [−WH] [−Obl]

     [$_{NP}$ e] left] was Fred]
     [wh]$_i$
     [−Obl]

In both (64a) and (64b), the [+THAT, −WH] SPEC will assign Case to the following trace, as is desired. In (64a), SPEC will prefix to the following trace, yielding a [e [e]] structure. If ∅ or "that" were inserted into the [+THAT, −WH] SPEC of (64a), the result would be ungrammatical, whether Prefixation applies or not. As noted in Chapter 3, the stipulation that lexical insertion must apply to *wh*-elements in [+THAT, −WH] SPECs rules out (64b) as a member of SS.

In conclusion, the distinction between the examples in (65), on the one hand, and (66), on the other, has been traced to the operation that moves "to" to the immediate right of certain verbs.

(65) (a) John wanted to leave town
    (b) Who did John want to leave town

(66) (a) *John believed to have left town
    (b) Who did John believe to have left town

Apparently this class of verbs is comprised largely of those verbs that select the FOR complementizer. Why this correlation should exist is not explained in this analysis. Work remains to be done, but this does not in itself cast doubt on the generalizations presented here.

The Rules of Construal for Reflexives and Reciprocals

An Analytic Option in the Statement of the Priority Filter

We have distinguished between "Move NP" (perhaps best thought of as *e*-Coindex) and the rules of construal for reflexives and reciprocals in Chapters 2 and 4. The motivation for the distinction involved, in part, the contrast between (67) and (68):

(67) $[_{NP_2}$ The men] showed $[_{NP_{(3,(2))}}$ the book] to

$[_{NP_2}$ each other]

(68) *$[_{NP_2}$ The men] showed $[_{NP_{(3,(2))}}$ the book] to $[_{NP_{(2,(2,3))}}$ e]

It was noted that if the NPs in (67) were to be analyzed as "alike" in terms of the Priority Filter, (67) would incorrectly be blocked. The option taken was to say that the Priority Filter Applies at PR (and, perhaps, SS), at which point the index of the NP that contains the reciprocal phrase would not yet have been assigned. Placing the rules of construal for reflexives and reciprocals within the set of rules determining the syntax of LF allows such structures to "finesse" the Priority Filter, as it were.

Structure (68), on the other hand, violates both the Priority Filter (since *e*-Coindex determines SS) and the i-set-i Filter.

There is another option to be examined. Suppose that the Priority Filter is altered in the following way:[10]

(69) *. . . B_i . . . A_j . . . A_i . . . , $i \neq j$
    where (i) B_i c-commands A_j and A_j c-commands A_i
       (ii) A_j and A_i are "alike"

Suppose further that "alikeness" is defined in such a way that A_j and A_i are "alike" only if *both* are *wh* (either *wh*-phrases or their traces), reflexive or reciprocal,[11] members of the element C (including their traces), and so on.

The fact that (68) violates both the Priority Filter and the i-set-i Filter suggests that we might wish to exclude $[_{NP}\, e]$ from the domain of the Priority Filter. This would eliminate a certain degree of overlap between the two filters. On the other hand, if the element usually referred to as "PRO" is to be identified with $[_{NP}\, e]$, as seems reasonable, given the marked nature of (70) as against (71) it would be best to accept the overlap between the two filters and include $[_{NP}\, e]$ in the domain of the Priority Filter.[12]

(70) $[_{NP_2}\, \text{John}]$ promised $[_{NP_{(3,\{2\})}}\, \text{Bill}][_{NP_2}\, e]$ to leave

(71) $[_{NP_2}\, \text{John}]$ persuaded $[_{NP_{(3,\{2\})}}\, \text{Bill}][_{NP_3}\, e]$ to leave

I wish to leave this question open here, however, and pursue the implications of (69) for the rules of construal for reflexives and reciprocals.

The formulation of the Priority Filter given in (69) would rule out a structure such as (72), assuming the appropriate c-command relations:

(72) . . . NP_i . . . $refl_j$ . . . $refl_i$ . . .

It is virtually impossible to construct a sentence in English of the structure of (72) which can be evaluated for a possible Priority Filter violation; virtually all such structures are in violation of independent constraints. The string (73) is impossible, but (74a) and (74b) are not significantly better, I believe.[13]

(73) *John gave Mary himself for herself

(74) (a) *John gave Mary a slave for herself
     (b) *John gave Mary himself for Susan

In Korean, however, the distribution of reflexives is much freer, and the implications of (69) can be assessed. Korean supports the reformulation. The translated sentence given in (75), for example, can only be construed as in (76a), not (76b).[14]

(75) [John [Bill [himself [himself Mary criticized]
believed] knows] believed]
"John believes Bill knows himself believed
himself criticized Mary"

(76) (a) (i) John$_i$ Bill$_j$ himself$_i$ himself$_i$
         (ii) John$_i$ Bill$_j$ himself$_j$ himself$_j$
     (b) (i) John$_i$ Bill$_j$ himself$_j$ himself$_i$
         (ii) John$_i$ Bill$_j$ himself$_i$ himself$_j$

Suppose that a (perhaps parameterized) version of (69) is correct. It would then be possible to index the reflexives and reciprocals, as well as *e*, by rules of construal at SS. The Priority Filter would then view all coindexed structures in a uniform way.

The Motivation for the Rules of Construal

As regards "forward" construal, the condition that the antecedent of a reflexive or reciprocal must c-command it is apparently without exception; the correct distinction between (77) and (78) is thereby made.

(77) $*[_{NP_2}[_{NP_3}$ John's] father] hit $[_{NP_3}$ himself]

(78) $[_{NP_2}[_{NP_3}$ John's] father] hit $[_{NP_2}$ himself]

The "c-command condition" is itself a reflex of the Binding Conditions; since $[_{NP_3}$ himself] is free(3) and in the domain of the subject, its referential index deletes and the impermissible NP_0 derived. Similarly, (79) is ruled out by the NIC.

(79) *himself left

Contrasts such as (80) argue for the necessity of a rule of construal for reflexives and reciprocals; neither reflexive undergoes the Binding Conditions, so it may be inferred that the fact that the reflexive has no construed antecedent is the source of its ungrammaticality.

(80) (a) $[_{NP_2}$ John] believed [that $[_{NP_3}$ pictures of

$[_{NP_2}$ himself]] were on sale]

(b) *[$_{NP_2}$ John] believed [that [$_{NP_3}$ pictures of

[$_{NP_4}$ himself]] were on sale]

The reflexive is free(4) in (80b), but is neither Nominative nor in the domain of the subject of NP$_3$, the minimal bounding node dominating it. Therefore, it appears that rules of construal for the reflexive and reciprocal have independent motivation in the assumed system; that examples such as (81) must also be ruled out shows the inadequacy of an alternative account of Opacity, in which the minimality condition is lifted, to the task of rendering the rules of construal superfluous.

(81) *Pictures of $\begin{Bmatrix} \text{themselves} \\ \text{each other} \end{Bmatrix}$ fell

A Note on "Backward" Construal

It is a curious and, to my knowledge, still unexplained fact that backward construal of reciprocals and reflexives violates the c-command condition.[15] The following examples show this:

(82) Pictures of [$_{NP_2}$ $\begin{Bmatrix} \text{themselves} \\ \text{each other} \end{Bmatrix}$][amused [$_{NP_2}$ the men]]

Although backward construal violates the c-command condition, it is by no means free, as the examples of (83) indicate.

(83) (a) *Pictures of [$_{NP_2}$ $\begin{Bmatrix} \text{themselves} \\ \text{each other} \end{Bmatrix}$][amused

[[$_{NP_2}$ the men's] friend]]

(b) *Pictures of [$_{NP_2}$ $\begin{Bmatrix} \text{themselves} \\ \text{each other} \end{Bmatrix}$] showed that

[$_{NP_2}$ they] had been mistreated

It would be sufficient for these examples to weaken the c-command condition for backward construal to Kommand.[16]

Kommand is apparently violated, however, by examples

such as the following:

(84) $[_S [_{SPEC} [_{NP}$ Which picture of herself $]]$

$[_S$ did $[_{NP}$ Mary$]$ see $[_{NP}$ e$]]]$

Yet a further relaxation of Kommand for the *wh*-Movement cases would not suffice to account for the felt contrast between (85a) and (85b) or (86a) and (86b).

(85) (a) ?Which picture of herself did Mary think
Bill had burned[17]
   (b) Which picture of himself did Mary think
Bill had burned

(86) (a) ?Which picture of herself did Mary persuade
Bill to burn
   (b) Which picture of herself did Mary promise
Bill to burn

The judgments in (85) and (86) parallel those in (87) and (88):

(87) (a) ?Mary thought Bill had burned a picture of herself
   (b) Mary thought Bill had burned a picture of himself

(88) (a) ?Mary persuaded Bill to burn a picture of herself
   (b) Mary promised Bill to burn a picture of herself

There is an alteration of the notion "trace" which yields a resolution of this problem.[18]

Suppose that the trace of a moved element contains all of the internal structure of that element, the sole difference between a trace and the element that binds it being that the phonological contents of trace are *e*. Under this assumption, "Bill" binds the reflexive in the trace of the *wh*-phrase in (85b), and the $[_{NP}$ e$]$ subject of the complement in (86b) does likewise. The reflexives in the moved *wh*-phrases may inherit the referential indices assigned within the traces they bind. The parallelism between the examples in (85) and (87), on the one hand, and (86) and (88), on the other, is thereby established.

Consider, in this light, the example in (89):

(89) $[_{NP_2}$ Pictures of $[_{NP_3}$ themselves$]]$ seemed

$[[_{NP_2}$ e] to please $[_{NP_3}$ the men]]

Again, the rule of construal applying to elements within trace allows (89) to parallel (90).

(90) $[_{NP_2}$ Pictures of $[_{NP_3}$ themselves]] please $[_{NP_2}$ the men]

Examples such as (90) remain as evidence that Kommand is a condition on backward construal.

As a last point, consider the structure in (91):

(91) *$[_{NP_2}$ Pictures of $[_{NP_3}$ e]] amused $[_{NP_3}$ the men]

How is (91) to be blocked?

Recall that anaphoric indices are assigned, under the proposed theory, to traces that are Cased, and note that the trace in (91) will receive Case from the preposition "of." I assume that in the circumstance of "backward" binding the structural conditions on the assignment of anaphoric indices parallel the structural conditions on the assignment of referential indices, as is true in the circumstance of "forward" binding. In backward binding, the structural condition, I believe, is Kommand. Thus, the trace in (91) will receive as members of its anaphoric index the referential index of each Kommanding NP. (92) will be produced:

(92) *$[_{NP_2}$ Pictures of $[_{NP_{(3,(3))}}$ e]] amused $[_{NP_3}$ the men]
$\phantom{(92) *[_{NP_2}$ Pictures of }$[+Obl]

But now we have an i-set-i Filter violation, which explains the ungrammaticality as desired.

The alteration of the notion "trace" proposed in this section, that a trace contains all of the internal structure of the constituent that binds it, further unifies the properties of a trace and its binder. In the case of NPs, we now note that if traces of NP are assigned all of the properties of non-pronominal non-anaphors such as "Bill," "destruction of Carthage," and so on, save that they have no phonological interpretation, it follows that they will be assigned Case and anaphoric indices, and will not undergo the Binding Conditions.

The Specificity of NPs

In Chapter 4, the topic of specificity was raised in the context of distinguishing between examples such as the following:

(93) Who did John see a picture of

(94) *Who did John see the picture of

I now wish to expand on this topic, beginning with a consideration of sentences such as (95) and (96):[19]

(95) John read his book

(96) John read his own book

The first point to note is that the examples in the pair (95) and (96) show, through the fact that they are both grammatical with intended coreference between the subject and the possessive pronoun, that the Indexing Algorithm of Chomsky (1978) is at least incomplete. For, in its application to (95), (97) is produced:[20]

(97) $[_{NP_2}$ John] read $[_{NP} [_{NP_{(3,(2))}}$ his] book]

Since "his" is neither Nominative nor in the domain of subject in the NP containing it, the anaphoric index of "his" will not delete, and the unwanted interpretation in which "John" and "his" may not be coreferential is forced.

In Fiengo and Higginbotham (forthcoming), this problem is resolved through appeal to an independent property distinguishing the NPs "his book" and "his own book." Since the pronoun "his" can serve as a referring expression, "his book" can denote a book. The NP "his own book" can be construed as having a denotation only relatively to an assignment of antecedent to the reflexive. Thus an NP like "his own book" is, in essence, an *open* NP, an NP with a free variable, while "his book" can be a *closed* NP. Let us call open NPs non-Specific, since they lack a determinate reference. We may now add to the Binding Conditions of Chomsky as follows:

(98) Suppose that α has designated index I and is free(i)
in β (β = NP or S) where:
(a) α is Nominative; or
(b) α is in the domain of subject of β; or
(c) α is properly contained in β, and β is Specific
Then I $\rightarrow$ 0 if I = i and I $\rightarrow$ I $-$ {i} if I is a set.

Returning to example (97), we may suppose that, since the possessive pronoun is referential, "his book" is a Specific NP. Consequently, the anaphoric index of "his" will delete as desired. In (99), however, the referential index of "his own" will not delete, since it is properly contained in a non-Specific NP.

(99) $[_{NP_2}$ John] read $[_{NP} [_{NP_2}$ his own] book]

The analysis extends to the examples in (100) and (101):

(100) John read books about him

(101) John read books about himself

Care must be taken to distinguish the various pronunciations of these examples; I focus here on what I believe to be the normal pronunciations (102) and (103):

(102) John read books about 'im

(103) John read books about 'imself

Assuming that plural NPs with $\emptyset$-determiners are non-Specific, as seems reasonable, we have the representations (105) and (106), which conform to intuition:

(104) $[_{NP_2}$ John] read $[_{NP}$ books about $[_{NP_{(3,(2))}}$ 'im]]

(105) $[_{NP_2}$ John] read $[_{NP}$ books about $[_{NP_2}$ 'imself]]

The generalization that bound anaphora is allowed just where disjoint reference is imposed is again obeyed.

The definiteness and the singularity of an NP both contribute to Specificity; in (106) and (107) the relevant contrast is reversed.

(106) *John read the book about 'imself

(107) <u>John</u> read the book about 'im

We may now return to the contrast given in (93) and (94). The possible SSs of (93) and (94) are as in (108) and (109); the (b) examples show the optional application of PP-Extraposition:

(108) (a) [$_{NP_2}$ who] John saw [$_{NP}$ a picture of [$_{NP_2}$ e]]

 (b) [$_{NP_2}$ who] John saw [$_{NP}$ a picture [$_{PP_3}$ e]]

 [$_{PP_3}$ of [$_{NP_2}$ e]]

(109) (a) [$_{NP_2}$ who] John saw [$_{NP}$ the picture of [$_{NP_2}$ e]]

 (b) [$_{NP_2}$ who] John saw [$_{NP}$ the picture [$_{PP_3}$ e]]

 [$_{PP_3}$ of [$_{NP_2}$ e]]

The (a) examples are ruled out by the NP Filter. Example (108b) is allowed. In (109b), however, the referential index of the trace PP in the Specific NP deletes, yielding the proscribed index 0. The contrast between (93) and (94) is explained.

Consider now the contrast between (110) and (111):

(110) Pictures of everybody are on my desk

(111) The picture of everybody is on my desk

Example (110) is ambiguous as regards the scope of the quantifier. The quantifier may have scope internal to the NP that contains it, in which interpretation each picture referred to is a picture of everybody, or the quantifier may have external scope, in which interpretation each person is such that pictures of him are on my desk.

The structure to be eliminated, therefore, is as in (112), where the rule of QR of May (1977a) has adjoined the quantifier "everybody" to S.

(112) [$_S$ [$_{NP_2}$ everybody][$_S$ [$_{NP}$ the picture of

 [$_{NP_2}$ e]] is on my desk]]

More precisely, the LF corresponding to (112) will be (113):

(113) [For every x, x a person][[the picture of x] is on my desk]

But the LF (114), which corresponds to (110), must be allowed:

(114) [For every x, x a person][[pictures of x] are on my desk]

The NP Filter, which applies at SS, is, of course, not responsible for the contrast between (113) and (114).

Suppose that we adopt the following Specificity Condition as a filter at LF:

> (115) *. . . x_i . . .
> if x_i is free(i) in a Specific NP

There are other pairs that illustrate the Specificity Condition; it applies in the (b) examples below:

(116) (a) We met men from everywhere
(b) We met the men from everywhere

(117) (a) Who read books about who
(b) Who read the books about who

(118) (a) They burned books in many languages
(b) They burned the books in many languages

The oddness of (116b) is due to the commonsense knowledge we have that no man is from everywhere; this is the internal scope reading forced by the Specificity Condition. The strangeness of (117b) derives from the fact that "who" cannot take internal scope. The only interpretation of (118b) is roughly synonymous to (119); again, this is the internal scope reading.

> (119) They burned the multilingual books

Returning to filter (115), recall that in Chapter 4 the possibility was raised that the Factivity Filter and the Specificity Condition might be identified. We return briefly to that topic here.

Suppose that (115) is recast as (120):

> (120) *. . . x_i . . .
> if (a) x_i is free(i) in a Specific NP
> or (b) x_i is free(i) in a Factive S

We have seen that various factors, among them definiteness and singularity, contribute to the specificity of an NP. These factors are structurally identifiable. The problem, then, is to identify those structural factors whose presence at LF would be sufficient to define the factives.

How are (121a) and (121b) to be distinguished?

    (121) (a) *Who was it remembered that Joe purged
            (b)   Who was it believed that Joe purged

I know of no structural distinction that one might exploit, short of ad hoc specifications.

Perhaps we see here not a distinction to be made at LF, but one to be made at SR. Assuming (what is to assume a great deal) that an appropriate metaphysics can be constructed in which states of affairs may be individuated and referred to, it is possible that the two cases of (120) might be collapsed at SR. But we now step beyond the concerns of this chapter, which were to examine the distinctions between SS and LF, on the one hand, and the rule system that relates them and the other rule systems in core grammar, on the other.[21]

Conclusion

In this chapter, as in Chapters 2 and 4, we have been concerned with assigning rules to their appropriate components, pointing out the implications of such choices for the level of SS. In art classes it is often given as an exercise to draw a figure, such as a tree, by representing only its background. The picture of SS that emerges here is largely composed in this manner. But we have also discovered certain quite general mechanisms that define the internal structure of SS and other levels. Nevertheless, the level SS remains vague in some respects. But it cannot be made more vivid in any other manner than by fixing the parameters of the rule systems that surround it; for its structure depends on the linguistic theory of which it is a part. Only as linguistic theory itself becomes more refined will our picture of SS become any more detailed.

Notes

References

Index

Notes

1. Introduction

1. As an extreme example, consider Plato's Socrates, who, considering astronomy to be analogous to geometry, advocated to Glaucon that they "let be the things in the heavens, if we are to have a part in the true science of astronomy" (*Republic VII*, 530c). The position is given a general expression in *Republic VII*, 529b,c: "But if anyone tries to learn about the things of sense, whether gaping up or looking down, I would never say that he really learns."

2. Concerning this point, see Chomsky (1975b), chapter 4, and for an alternative perspective on the topic, Planck (1949).

3. See Chomsky (1975a, 1975b) for discussion of the nature of an autonomy thesis and the part that such a conception plays in the pursuit of linguistics as an empirical science.

4. See Chomsky (1972) and Postal (1972).

5. See Chomsky (1975b), chapter 4, and, for more general discussion, see Chomsky (1977a, 1977b).

6. For a more general treatment of the topics addressed here, see Fiengo (forthcoming).

7. It would be out of place here to focus attention on the specific analytic claims and assumptions that this paragraph contains. The usefulness of this position to our discussion resides, rather, in that it provides methodological contrasts to the program adopted in the present volume. See Block and Dworkin (1976) for discussion. It might be claimed that a reduction is effected by such an operational definition, but this is surely false. See Popper (1963), p. 278, for a discussion of this matter.

8. As Kuhn points out, the scientist "who builds an instrument to determine optical wave lengths must not be satisfied with a piece of equipment that merely attributes particular numbers to particular spectral lines. He is not just an explorer or measurer. On the contrary, he must show, by analyzing his apparatus in terms of the established body of optical theory, that the numbers his instrument produces are the ones that enter theory as wave lengths" (Kuhn, 1962, p. 35). Contrast this with Jensen's observation that "there is no point in arguing the question to which there is no answer, the question of what intelligence *really* is. The best we can do is to obtain measurements of certain kinds of behavior and look at their relationships to other phenomena and see if these relationships make any kind of sense and order" (Jensen, 1972, p. 73). It is of interest to note that a similar sort of analytic limitation can be recognized in the attempt to construct procedures for determining the phonemic inventory of a language.

9. See Lakoff (1971), for such examples.

10. For formulations of the first, see Katz and Postal (1964), Chomsky (1965); for formulations of the second, see Chomsky (1971), Jackendoff (1972); for formulations of the third, see Chomsky (1975b), Fiengo (1974, 1977), Chomsky and Lasnik (1977), among others.

11. Thus I follow Chomsky (1970) in my use of the term "deep structure."

12. I abstract away here, and later, from the possibility that other levels in the derivation, e.g., end-of-cycle, are semantically interpreted, as suggested in Jackendoff (1972) and Fiengo and Lasnik (1973).

13. This matter is discussed in Katz (1976); however, the distinction between "benign" and "malignant" global mechanisms discussed here is not effected. Assuming all global mechanisms to be malignant, Katz concludes, incorrectly I believe, that EST is less restrictive. As I have tried to indicate, this is not necessarily so.

14. For an analysis of these matters which makes these assumptions, see Fiengo and Lasnik (1973).

15. The relation is slightly more complex than indicated, as shown in Fiengo and Lasnik (1973) and Fiengo (1974). The added complexity is not such as would give solace to the proponent of deep structure interpretation of these examples, however.

16. See, for example, Chomsky and Lasnik (1978) and related work.

2. Movement and Hopping

1. See also Postal (1972), where a different answer to our question is presented.

2. For a more detailed presentation of this example, see Higginbotham and Fiengo (in preparation).

3. There is also the nominal "destruction of Carthage by Rome." In previous works (Fiengo, 1974, 1977) I argued that the initial trace in the derivation of this nominal is replaced by a zero determiner. The argu-

ment was that this yielded a maximally simple statement of the distribution of determiners for reasons independent of NP-Movement, although
the analysis of the distribution of trace defended there (and here) required
that no trace could precede the NP it is coindexed with at SS. This was
the theory that traces must be "properly bound," that is, preceded by
their coindexed NP. Bach (1977) complains, however, that he "find[s]
this analysis completely unconvincing and ad hoc and conclude[s] that if
trace theory is right, then that analysis is wrong." In response, I wish to
state first that I know of no simpler analysis of nominals lacking overt
determiners in the literature. Since in the present volume it is assumed
that lexical insertion is at SS, the rule spelling out determiners is simply a
rule of lexical insertion. This simple proposal also satisfies questions
raised in Dresher and Hornstein (1979). As for Bach's inference that if
trace theory is right, this analysis is wrong, I find it puzzling.

4. I follow here the system presented in Chomsky (1970).

5. See M. Anderson (1978), where this generalization is independently observed.

6. I assume that in nominals such as "a book by John," "John" is
correctly assigned by [+affect], as the author of the book. Contrast in
this regard "Roget's thesaurus" and "a thesaurus by Roget," where only
the second unambiguously attributes authorship to Roget.

7. This proposal contrasts with those of Fillmore (1968), Gruber (1965,
1967), and Jackendoff (1972), among others.

8. The theory of Case presented here follows suggestions by Jean-
Roger Vergnaud and Chomsky (1978) but differs in execution from these
proposals. With the exception of the Possessive, only the pronominal
system shows the full Case paradigm, "her/him" being Oblique and
"she/he" being Nominative, etc.

9. α c-commands β if the first branching node dominating α dominates β. See Reinhart (1976, 1978). I assume further that if α dominates β
it does not c-command β and that no node c-commands itself.

10. A sentence such as "he left" will be analyzed as having a $\emptyset$ allomorph of *that* in its COMP. Sentences such as "I know who he saw"
are discussed in Chapter 3.

11. More explicitly, consider a structure such as (i), where the trace of
the *wh*-phrase is assigned Case by the usual mechanisms:

$$(i) \ldots [_i wh\text{-phrase}] \ldots [_i e] \ldots$$
$$[\alpha \text{Oblique}]$$

(i) will be rewritten, by convention, as (ii):

$$(ii) \ldots [_i wh\text{-phrase}] \ldots [_i e] \ldots$$
$$[\alpha \text{Oblique}] \qquad [\alpha \text{Oblique}]$$

The features of Case are probably not alone in undergoing this copying
process.

$$(iii) [_i \text{Which men}] \text{ did John know } e_i$$

Such examples as (iii) probably are to be assigned their stress patterns by copying the primary stress features assigned to the trace of the *wh*-phrase onto the *wh*-phrase itself.

12. There are, to be sure, examples such as "John was looked at," but "looked at" is here an adjective, as in "a frequently looked at painting."

13. See Fiengo (1974, 1977) for the relevant argumentation, as well as Chomsky (1975a).

14. See Fiengo (1977).

15. I will refer to this as the "*N Filter," the statement being:

*. . . N . . . where N is lexical and has no Case

See Chomsky (1978) for this proposal.

16. This may explain how in a sentence like "I gave Fido a bone," "a bone" receives Case. If "gave Fido" is not a V, as seems likely, we can say that since "give" subcategorizes two NPs, it assigns Case to these NPs. This in turn suggests that government might be dropped as a condition on the assignment of Oblique Case.

17. See Emonds (1976), p. 82.

18. It is critical that the string "a schedule to the stockholders" not be analyzed as a constituent. An example such as (i) forces the relevant structure:

(i) *The secretary sent it to the stockholders out (from the office)

19. See Fiengo and Battistella (in preparation) for discussion of these options.

20. See Chomsky (1965), p. 180ff.

21. That is, that these suffixes may not appear at the level of PR unless they are attached to a stem; see Chapter 3. Interestingly, it appears that the Case suffix is sometimes copied onto an NP from another NP in the sentence. Note that we have "I know who John is," but never *"I know whom John is," suggesting that the position following "is" in "John is a cook" is assigned Nominative Case by a rule that copies the Case of the subject onto this position (see Edwards (1980), where the intimate involvement of Case and anaphora in equative sentences is discussed). It might be suggested that there is a well-defined set of features that can be inserted into lexical items; if this is so, the redundancy between rules (148) and (157) could be eliminated by dropping rule (157).

22. I abstract away here from the occurrence of "not" in such constructions as "not many men," "he thought not," "not that I care," and so on.

23. It appears optimal to consider "to" a member of the category [+V, −N, +AUX]^0.

24. I make the assumption here that only rules within the lexicon can state generalizations concerning the internal structure of lexical items. While the rules of inflectional morphology, such as the Suffixation rule, may combine morphemes to form words, they may not analyze the internal morphological structure of lexical items.

25. There are subcategorizational dependencies between TNS and the choice of complementizer; these questions are addressed in Fiengo and Battistella (in preparation).

26. The impossibility of "mayn't" is apparently idiosyncratic. The same point can be made using *"John couldn't had left."

27. One possibility would be to analyze the string TNS NOT as having the structure:

$$\text{(i)} \quad [_{\text{TNS}} \text{ TNS NOT}]$$

There would, on this analysis, be two featurally nondistinct elements TNS, one in construction with NOT, the other dominating TNS NOT. The prohibition against the "same" element C undergoing Hop C twice would not be able to distinguish the two elements TNS, as desired.

28. The element "to," like the modals, must apparently be assigned the $\emptyset$ affix as well; there are alternatives to be explored here, however.

29. This principle, which I will call the Affix Principle, is developed in Chapter 3.

30. This distribution serves as evidence for my statement earlier that "subjunctives" lack TNS. The question is of interest, recall, since it casts doubt on the contention that TNS assigns Nominative Case.

31. There is a similar problem in stating the distribution of the hopping of AUX. The well-known contrast between (i) and (ii) suggests that the scope of the negative is relevant:

(i) (a) On not many occasions, he has cried
   (b) On not many occasions has he cried

(ii) (a) *Not on many occasions, he has cried
   (b) Not on many occasions has he cried

The possibility exists that these facts, as well as the facts of Quantifier movement, require that our prohibition against global mechanisms be relaxed.

3. Complementizer Allomorphy

1. See, for example, Chomsky and Lasnik (1977), and for an analysis with different metatheoretical assumptions, Bresnan (1972).

2. As is pointed out, for example, in Bach and Horn (1976), pronouns may not take adjuncts or complements, under normal circumstances. Thus the ungrammaticality of an example such as (3a) argues that the only syntactic analysis positions "to write with" as an adjunct of "it"—prohibited under the assumed generalization.

3. The oddness of (8b) apparently derives, then, from the oddness of the concept that the purpose of a friend is to play with that person.

4. The examples in (9) also have a reading in which the head of the relative clause is interpreted to be the *ne plus ultra* of its class. What relation this fact has to the purposiveness of the relative clause is unclear to me.

5. This construction, and those preceding, should be carefully distinguished from cases of "double control," where a relative clause structure is inappropriate. (i) is an example; see Chomsky (1978) for discussion.

(i) John bought the dog to play with

As has often been noted (e.g., in Chomsky and Lasnik (1977)), relative infinitivals in which the subject has been relativized are sometimes odd:

(ii) ?A man to do the job walked in

Since replacement of the indefinite by the definite article seems to render the structure perfectly grammatical, I do not believe the strangeness of (ii) is due to structural considerations.

6. This argument is irrelevant, of course, if the *wh*-Movement analysis of Chomsky (1977e) is assumed.

7. Example (32) contrasts with Object Deletion sentences such as (i), and example (33a) contrasts with (ii).

(i) *That topic is too trivial for there to be any disagreement about

(ii) *Max is too stingy (for you) to be employed by

See Lasnik and Fiengo (1974).

8. See Chomsky (1977e), in particular, the discussion concerning his (106c) and (106d).

9. In fact, I assume that all preterminal elements are expanded as *e* by the PS-rules.

10. The structures in (44) are the equivalent of Chomsky and Lasnik (1977), example (51).

11. See the section on ∅-Allomorphy for some implications of this assumption.

12. In these and the following bracketings, the feature [±WH] is used as a featural opposition within the SPEC (COMP) node, as in Chomsky (1977c). [wh], on the other hand, is a feature of a nonterminal node dominating a *wh*-word. Nodes that contain this feature are moved by *wh*-Movement. [−WH] underlies relatives, *that*-clauses, *for*-clauses, etc.

13. I make the simplifying assumption here that the insertion of the complementizer elements follows the other insertions. Once the general theory is presented, it will be seen that this assumption is unnecessary. I am not assuming that there are distinct rules of *for*-Insertion and *wh*-Insertion, necessarily.

14. See Chomsky and Halle (1968), p. 369. For an alternative suggestion, compare Liberman and Prince (1977), p. 328.

15. Terry Langendoen has brought to my attention a counterexample to the AP which Bloomfield cites in his "Menomini Morphophonemics: "Throughout the morphology, zero suffixes must sometimes be set up. It is a striking feature of Algonquian that in certain cases we must set up the root of a word as zero. In a few verb forms the stem is replaced by zero; thus, the stem ɛn-'say so to' is replaced by zero before the inflec-

tional suffix -ðk-: enéw 'he says so to him,' ekwāh 'the other says so to him,' netékwah 'he says so to me.' A large class of noun stems and certain particles contain no root and occur only with the prefixes of §7: these are *dependent* nouns and particles, such as -nɛhk-, -ēyaw-, -ōhn-, in §7, or, say (with two suffixes), -ēt-aʔnɛmw- in kétaʔnɛm 'thy fellow-cur,' wētaʔnɛmon 'his fellow-cur'" (Bloomfield, 1970, p. 355). Why Algonquian should behave this way I have no idea. That Bloomfield found the fact striking suggests that he assumed some form of the AP himself.

16. Here it is assumed that the application of Prefixation is obligatory. For a better alternative, see the section on trace and "PRO" subjects later in this chapter.

17. I will continue to use capitals to refer to morphemes, minuscules to refer to their allomorphs.

18. For many people, if Ø is replaced by "for" in (77b), the result is still ungrammatical. The impossibility of the Ø-allomorph of FOR following NP is also illustrated with an example from relative infinitivals:

(i) A pen $\begin{Bmatrix} \text{for} \\ *\emptyset \end{Bmatrix}$ John to write with was on the table

19. The definition of "bound" will be returned to below, and (82) will be refined.

20. For suggestive analyses of these and related facts, see Bresnan (1971) and Selkirk (1972).

21. In some of these examples, e.g., "he waited for John to leave," the "for" might be analyzed either as the complementizer or the preposition. In the example in (i), we have both:

(i) What I waited for was for John to leave

Even if it is the complementizer that is analyzed as having a Ø-allomorph in examples such as "he waited for John to leave," it is clear that the presence of the Ø-allomorph is marked.

22. This filter is example 68 of Chomsky and Lasnik (1977).

23. See Maling and Zaenen (1978), pp. 478–480.

24. The grammaticality of Ozark examples such as those in (i) suggests that "for" can be free in that dialect; I know of no independent evidence for this, however.

(i) (a) It is wrong for to do that
    (b) Who are you going to try for to go to the church social with you

25. This resolution was suggested to me by Edwin Battistella.

26. The stipulation must be that [+THAT] *wh*-NPs must undergo lexical insertion (in SPEC positions) to prevent *"a pen which to write with," *"a man who to talk to" from being forced. The SPECs in these examples will be [−THAT], of course. The stipulation given is, correctly, without generality or analytic depth; Black English, in which "the man left" is a possible relative clause construction, lacks this stipulation.

27. Note, however, that the fact that there are complementizers that may stand as free morphemes poses a problem, since they of course do not undergo Hop C. Perhaps it is best to state, therefore, that no specifiers may belong to C; this renders the Prefixation Hypothesis superfluous with respect to the inability of the intrinsically bound complementizers to hop, but not with respect to the "that-trace" phenomena, and so forth.

4. Filters on Anaphora Patterns

1. Here, and in all the examples following, it is crucial that the sentences not be read with contrastive stress or with the intonation of a question. Sentence (ib), for example, is perfectly acceptable if "who" is given "echo" status:

> (i) (a) Q: What did the Wizard of Oz see?
> (b) Echo Q: What did who see!?

The distribution of echo-*wh*-words, though an interesting topic in its own right, is not the subject of the present investigation.

2. Superiority is defined as follows: "Category *A* is 'superior' to category *B* in the phrase marker if every major category dominating *A* dominates *B* as well but not conversely . . ." (Chomsky, 1977c, p. 101). In a footnote to this passage, Chomsky presents a "slightly extended" notion of "superior" in order to accommodate certain facts related to *each*-Movement (see Chomsky, 1977c, footnote 27). The choice between these two formulations is not relevant to the criticism of the Superiority Condition given here, which applies equally to both of them.

With respect to the notion "major category," Chomsky states: "We use the term 'major category' in the sense of Chomsky (1965, p. 74), that is, N, V, A and the categories that dominate them" (Chomsky, 1977c, footnote 27). Crucially, as will be seen, P and PP are not major categories in Chomsky's framework.

It is relevant to note that the Superiority Condition remains in later elaborations of linguistic theory—see Chomsky (1977e), footnote 20, and the associated text.

3. (8) is example (73) in Chomsky (1977c).

4. (9) is example (75) in Chomsky (1977c).

5. (10) is example (76) in Chomsky (1977c).

6. I assume, with Freidin (1978), that the (strict) cycle can, in effect, be derived from other independently motivated conditions and that it therefore plays no role in ruling out examples such as (11b) and (12b). I also believe, however, as will become clear, that subjacency plays no role.

7. I use the notation [wh] as a feature on nodes which can be moved by *wh*-Movement. It is not to be confused with the feature [±WH], which is an opposition within COMP only.

8. If structures such as $[_{VP}$ V PP NP] are allowed, it appears to be

necessary to adopt the theory discussed in Chapter 2 that V may assign Case to any NP that it is subcategorized for, whether adjacent or not. The task of eliminating such examples as *"John gave to Bill a book" devolves, appropriately, I believe, to the principles that measure relative "heaviness" of elements within VP. See Fiengo (1977) for discussion.

9. It might be objected that (23b) is not a possible underlying structure because of the impossibility of examples such as (i):

(i) *Who gave to whom what

This objection is not to the point, however, since there are conditions on constituent order within VP (e.g., "heaviness," as pointed out in note 8) which apply at the level of PR, after *wh*-Movement has applied. Similar remarks obtain for (24a) and (a') below.

Note, furthermore, that when a final *wh*-phrase of sufficient heaviness is replaced for "what" in (i), the result is grammatical:

(ii) Who gave to whom what books about logic

There seems to be no doubt, therefore, that there exist underlying structures such as (23b); indeed, it would be an unnecessary complication to exclude (23b) while allowing (ii), given the independent necessity of a filter sensitive to heaviness.

The impossibility of examples such as (iii) is not relevant to the Priority Filter, as the example in (iv) shows:

(iii) *Who did John give to _____ what

(iv) *Who did John give to _____ those books about logic

10. Node A "c-commands" node B if neither A nor B dominates the other and the first branching node that dominates A dominates B. (See Reinhart, 1976.) I assume that PP counts in the statement of c-command.

11. This type of sentence, and the relevant observations concerning it, are originally due, I believe, to Kayne.

12. Similar comments obtain regarding the assignment of indices to the reflexive, as well as the "Equi site." An SS such as (i), will, in particular, not contain an *e* coindexed with "John" (but see the section on the NP Filter contrasted with the Specificity Condition).

(i) John promised Bill [e to leave]

Note also that a counterexample of the form (ii) is only an apparent one if it is assumed either that (ii) derives from (iii) by a rule that applies in the component relating SS and PR, or that the c-command condition on the Priority Filter is correct (see the section on the NP Filter).

(ii) $John_i$ seems to the man_j [e_i to be crazy]

(iii) $John_i$ seems [e_i to be crazy] to the man_j

13. See Chomsky (1977e), p. 108.

14. It is crucial, due to the fact that adjectives do not assign Case, to assume that "of" is part of the same constituent as "taken advantage."

15. If an NP has an anaphoric index, that is its designated index; otherwise, the referential index of an NP is its designated index. I assume that reflexives and reciprocals do not receive anaphoric indices; therefore the designated index of these forms is always the referential index. (See Chapter 5 for discussion.)

16. The point is that in structures such as (79b), e_i is not "properly bound" in the sense of Fiengo (1974, 1977).

17. I wish to refer the reader to the excellent study by Guéron (1978) in which many of the complexities of the PP-Extraposition process are dealt with.

18. In Chomsky's system this rule is lexically governed. Note that if surface structure lexical insertion is assumed, government as a restriction on application can be transposed into normal properties of subcategorization. The relative ordering of the Readjustment Rule and *wh*-Movement seems to be without consequence for this example; under either ordering, structure (i) will be generated.

$$\text{(i) } who_j \ldots [_{NP} \ldots e_i \ldots]_{PP_i} \ldots e_j \ldots] \ldots$$

Note that while the anaphoric relation of the *wh*-word and its trace does not violate a symmetrical NP Filter, the Readjustment Rule, here formulated as an instance of "vacuous" extraposition, does. It is possible that the Readjustment Rule should be formulated not as an extraction but as a rebracketing, i.e., a movement of brackets. Under this analysis, the symmetrical statement of the NP Filter would not be negated by these examples. (73b) would be replaced by (ii):

$$\text{(ii) He saw } [_{NP} \text{ a picture}][_{PP} \text{ of John}]$$

However, we will see in the section on the Specificity Condition that an extraposition analysis is preferable.

19. Of course, if the NP Filter is formulated as only conditioning outputs of leftward movement, it is sufficient to block *wh*-Movement applications in the desired way:

$$\text{(i) *Who}_i \text{ does John remember } [_{NP} \text{ the fact that Bill hates } e_i]$$

$$\text{(ii) *Whose}_i \text{ did you read } [_{NP} e_i \text{ book}]$$

$$\text{(iii) *Who}_i \text{ did } [_{NP} \text{ a friend of } e_i] \text{ hate Fred}$$

The filter also subsumes A-over-A violations by leftward NP-Movement applications.

20. For an extended argument along these same lines, see Koster (1978).

21. This convention is later altered in that article in ways that are not relevant here.

22. The "double NP" constructions raise two interesting problems, which I wish to discuss here. First, how is Case to be assigned in an example such as (i)?

(i) John$_i$ was [$_A$ given] e$_i$ [a book]

There appears to be no appropriate governor for the NP "a book."

Recall that in an example such (ii) it was proposed (in Chapter 2) that Case is assigned to both NPs by virtue of the fact that "give" is subcategorized for them.

(ii) John gave [$_{NP}$ Bill][$_{NP}$ a book]

Suppose, then, that we give this proposal full generality, stating that both "give" and "given," since they together are subcategorized for the double NP construction, assign Case to the two NPs. The problem now becomes that of ruling out (iiia) and (iiib):

(iii) (a) John was given Bill a book

(b) [$_{NP_i}$ John] was given [$_{NP_{(i,ii)}}$ e][a book]
   [Obl]

Consequently, we may now propose the following rule of Case deletion:

(iv) Case → ∅ / . . . A ——— . . .

This rule deletes Case only from an NP immediately to the right of an adjective. Presumably, (iv) should be generalized to (v) to account for examples such as (vi):

(v) Case → ∅ / . . . [+N]——— . . .

(vi) *Rome's destruction Carthage

It appears that, given (v), no other statement regarding Case specific to adjectives and nouns need be made. The middle construction, whose verbs seem to have the subcategorizational properties of adjectives, as noted in Chapter 2, will fall under (V), since [+N] is to be interpreted as the subcategorization feature of the constituent. In the normal case, this will correspond to its syntactic shape, as in (i), but in marked constructions such as the middle, variation is allowed.

The second problem raised by the "double NP" involves the following pair of sentences:

(vii) (a) What did you give who
    (b) Who did you give what

I find the first example somewhat worse than the second; the contrast is even greater in the following pairs:

(viii) (a) What did you send who
    (b) Who did you send what

(ix) (a) What did you throw who
    (b) Who did you throw what

The Priority Filter would require that the (a) examples in these pairs be ungrammatical, but their status seems only intermediate, whence the problem. Furthermore, the (b) examples above seem to be somewhat better than the examples in (x):

(x) Who did you $\begin{cases} \text{give} \\ \text{send} \\ \text{throw} \end{cases}$ a book

Worst of all, however, are the examples in (xi):

(xi) Who did you $\begin{cases} \text{give} \\ \text{send} \\ \text{throw} \end{cases}$ it

The ungrammaticality of examples such as (xi) is discussed in the text; that the (b) examples of (viii) and (ix) are not as ungrammatical as (xii) remains a problem.

(xii) What did who hit

23. See Fiengo and Higginbotham (forthcoming) for a comprehensive discussion of these topics.

24. This topic will be pursued in Chapter 5.

25. There is a vexing problem as regards disjoint reference between NPs in VP. Consider the contrast in (i):

(i) (a) He talked to Mary about her
   (b) *He talked to her about Mary

Although "her" does not c-command "Mary" in (i)b, if PP is included in the branching nodes with respect to which c-command is defined, it nevertheless is disjoint in reference from it.

5. Topics in the Syntax of Logical Form

1. In Chapter 4, it was argued that PRO might be identified with trace, receiving its index by a rule coindexing e. If this is true, there need be no independent rule of construal for PRO. See the section on variables and control for further discussion.

2. See Chomsky (1978), Appendix.

3. See Chomsky (1978), Appendix.

4. The domain of a node is the nodes that it c-commands. β is the minimal node containing α if there is no δ contained by β and containing α, where β and δ are NP or S.

5. May states the Condition on Quantifier Binding as follows: "Every quantified phrase must properly bind a variable" (May, 1977a, p. 22).

6. In Chomsky (1975b), these are referred to as the SR-2 rules, which operate on LF to yield "meaning," which depends also on other systems that are extragrammatical.

7. This requirement will be expanded below.

8. See May (1978), in which an analysis roughly along the lines presented here is first presented. Many of the problems raised in Pullum (1979) are handled either on my account or that of May.

9. As pointed out in Bresnan (1972).

10. This formalization is, I believe, essentially the "Minimal Distance Principle" of Rosenbaum (1967) and C. Chomsky (1969). It crucially differs from the proposal of Koster (1978), the Locality Principle, in that the Priority Filter is an "intervention" constraint in his sense, while the Locality Principle is not.

11. I leave open the question of whether the reflexive is alike to the reciprocal.

12. I see no reason to preclude the overlap of two general conditions as a matter of principle. It is simple to imagine circumstances in which a prohibition against overlap would force one to complicate general conditions. While massive overlap is suspicious, it is only so since it suggests that a simpler account with fewer general conditions is attainable.

13. Gender, of course, does not count with respect to alikeness.

14. See Fiengo and Kim (in preparation).

15. By the term "c-command condition" I refer to the condition, presumably to be stated at LF, that anaphors must be c-commanded by the NPs to which they are coindexed. See Reinhart (1976).

16. The term is Lasnik's (1976). A Kommands B if the minimal cyclic node (NP or S) dominating A also dominates B.

17. In this and the following examples, care should be taken not to stress the reflexive; the stressed reflexive has distinct anaphoric properties.

18. The notion that follows was suggested to me by Noam Chomsky, although not in this context.

19. See Fiengo and Higginbotham (forthcoming) for a more complete presentation.

20. Irrelevant indices are suppressed.

21. I will accept the advice of De Morgan, who wrote: "I would not dissuade a student from metaphysical inquiry; on the contrary, I would rather endeavour to promote the desire of entering upon such subjects: but I would warn him, when he tries to look down his own throat with a candle in his hand, to take care that he does not set his head on fire" (De Morgan, 1926, p. 30).

References

Akmajian, A. 1975. More evidence for an NP cycle. *Linguistic Inquiry* 6:115–129.

Anderson, M. 1978. Transformations in noun phrases. University of Connecticut (mimeographed).

Anderson, S. R. 1977. Comments on the paper by Wasow. In *Formal syntax*, ed. P. Culicover, T. Wasow, and A. Akmajian. New York: Academic Press.

Arnauld, A., and C. Lancelot. 1975. *The Port-Royal grammar*, ed. J. Rieux and B. Rollin. The Hague: Mouton.

Bach, E. 1977. Comments on the paper by Chomsky. In *Formal syntax*, ed. P. Culicover, T. Wasow, and A. Akmajian. New York: Academic Press.

Bach, E., and G. Horn. 1976. Remarks on 'Conditions on transformations.' *Linguistic Inquiry* 7:265–299.

Block, N. J., and G. Dworkin. 1976. I.Q., hereditability, and inequality. In *The I.Q. controversy*, ed. N. J. Block and G. Dworkin. New York: Pantheon.

Bloomfield, L. 1970. Menomini morphophonemics. In *A Leonard Bloomfield anthology*, ed. C. Hockett. Bloomington: Indiana University Press.

Bresnan, J. 1971. On sentence stress and syntactic transformations. *Language* 47:257–281.

———. 1972. Theory of complementation in English syntax. Doctoral dissertation, Massachusetts Institute of Technology.

———. 1978. A realistic transformational grammar. In *Linguistic theory and psychological reality*, ed. M. Halle, J. Bresnan, and G. Miller. Cambridge, Mass.: MIT Press.

CHOMSKY, C. 1969. *The acquisition of syntax in children from 5 to 10.* Cambridge, Mass.: MIT Press.

CHOMSKY, N. 1965. *Aspects of the theory of syntax.* Cambridge, Mass.: MIT Press.

———. 1970. Remarks on nominalization. In *Readings in English transformational grammar,* ed. R. Jacobs and P. Rosenbaum. Waltham, Mass.: Ginn.

———. 1971. Deep structure, surface structure, and semantic interpretation. In *Semantics,* ed. D. Steinberg and L. Jakobovits. Cambridge: Cambridge University Press.

———. 1972. Some empirical issues in the theory of transformations. In *Goals of linguistic theory,* ed. S. Peters. Englewood Cliffs, N.J.: Prentice-Hall.

———. 1977a. Questions of form and interpretation. In *Essays on form and interpretation.* New York: North Holland.

———. 1977b. On the nature of language. In *Essays on form and interpretation.* New York: North Holland.

———. 1977c. Conditions on transformations. In *Essays on form and interpretation.* New York: North Holland.

———. 1977d. Conditions on rules of grammar. In *Essays on form and interpretation.* New York: North Holland.

———. 1977e. On Wh-movement. In *Formal Syntax,* ed. P. Culicover, T. Wasow, and A. Akmajian. New York: Academic Press.

———. 1978. On binding (to appear in *Linguistic Inquiry*).

CHOMSKY, N., and M. HALLE. 1968. The sound pattern of English. New York: Harper & Row.

CHOMSKY, N., and H. LASNIK. 1977. Filters and control. *Linguistic Inquiry* 8:425–504.

———. 1978. A remark on contraction. *Linguistic Inquiry* 9:268–274.

DE MORGAN, A. 1926. *Formal logic,* ed. A. E. Taylor. London: Open Court Company.

DRESHER, B. E., and N. HORNSTEIN. 1979. Trace theory and NP movement rules. *Linguistic Inquiry* 10:65–82.

EDWARDS, J. 1980. Equatives: some preliminary considerations (mimeographed).

EMONDS, J. 1976. *A transformational approach to English syntax.* New York: Academic Press.

———. 1977. Comments on the paper by Lightfoot. In *Formal syntax,* ed. P. Culicover, T. Wasow, and A. Akmajian. New York: Academic Press.

FIENGO, R. 1974. Semantic conditions on surface structure. Doctoral dissertation, Massachusetts Institute of Technology.

———. 1977. On trace theory. *Linguistic Inquiry* 8:35–81.

——— (forthcoming). On "having Language."

FIENGO, R., and E. BATTISTELLA (in preparation). Specifier dependencies.

FIENGO, R., and J. HIGGINBOTHAM (forthcoming). Opacity in NP.

FIENGO, R., and H. KIM (in preparation). Korean anaphora.

FIENGO, R., and H. Lasnik. 1973. Logical structure of reciprocal sentences. *Foundations of Language* 9:447–468.

––––––. 1976. Some issues in the theory of transformations. *Linguistic Inquiry* 7:182–191.

Fillmore, C. 1968. The case for case. In *Universals in linguistic theory*, ed. E. Bach and R. Harms. New York: Holt, Rinehart and Winston.

FREIDIN, R. 1978. Cyclicity and the theory of grammar. *Linguistic Inquiry* 9:519–549.

GRUBER, J. 1965. *Studies in lexical relations*. Doctoral dissertation, Massachusetts Institute of Technology. Bloomington: Indiana University Linguistics Club.

GRUBER, J. 1967. *Functions of the lexicon in formal descriptive grammar*. Santa Monica: Systems Development Corporation, TM-3770/000/00.

GUÉRON, J. 1978. The grammar of PP extraposition (mimeographed).

HAMILTON, E., and H. CAIRNS, eds. 1961. *Plato: The collected dialogues*. New York: Bollingen Foundation.

HIGGINBOTHAM, J. (in press). Pronouns and bound variables. *Linguistic Inquiry*.

–––––– (forthcoming). On questions.

HIGGINBOTHAM, J., and R. FIENGO (in preparation). On psychological reality.

HIGGINBOTHAM, J., and R. MAY. 1979a. A general theory of crossing coreference. *Proceedings of NELS IX*. New York: City University of New York.

––––––. 1979b. Crossing, markedness, pragmatics. Paper presented at the 4th Annual GLOW Colloquium, Pisa, Italy. (To appear in colloquium proceedings.)

–––––– (in press). Questions, quantifiers, and crossing. *Linguistic Review*.

HORNSTEIN, N. 1977. S and X̄ convention. *Linguistic Analysis* 3:137–176.

JACOB, F. 1973. *The logic of life: A history of heredity*. New York: Pantheon.

JACKENDOFF, R. 1972. *Semantic interpretation in generative grammar*. Cambridge, Mass.: MIT Press.

JENSEN, A. R. 1972. How much can we boost IQ and scholastic achievement? In *Genetics and education*. New York: Harper & Row.

KATZ, J. 1976. Global rules and surface structure. In *An integrated theory of linguistic ability*, ed. T. Bever, J. Katz, and D. T. Langendoen. New York: Crowell.

KATZ, J., and P. POSTAL. 1964. *An integrated theory of linguistic description*. Cambridge, Mass.: MIT Press.

KAYNE, R. S. 1975. *French syntax*. Cambridge, Mass.: MIT Press.

KIPARSKY, P., and C. KIPARSKY. 1970. Fact. In *Progress in linguistics*, ed. M. Bierwisch and K. Heidolph. The Hague: Mouton.

KOSTER, J. 1978. *Locality principles in syntax*. Dordrecht: Foris Publications.

KUHN, T. 1962. *The structure of scientific revolutions*. Chicago: University of Chicago Press.

LAKOFF, G. 1971. On generative semantics. In *Semantics: An interdisciplinary reader in philosophy, linguistics and psychology*, ed. D. Steinberg and L. Jakobovits. Cambridge: Cambridge University Press.

LASNIK, H. 1976. Remarks on coreference. *Linguistic Analysis* 2:1–22.

LASNIK, H., and R. FIENGO. 1974. Complement object deletion. *Linguistic Inquiry* 5:559–582.

LIBERMAN, M., and A. PRINCE. 1977. On stress and linguistic rhythm. *Linguistic Inquiry* 8:249–336.

LIGHTFOOT, D. 1977. On traces and conditions on rules. In *Formal syntax*, ed. P. Culicover, T. Wasow, and A. Akmajian. New York: Academic Press.

MALING, J., and A. ZAENEN. 1978. The nonuniversality of a surface filter. *Linguistic Inquiry* 9:475–497.

MAY, R. 1977a. The grammar of quantification. Doctoral dissertation, Massachusetts Institute of Technology.

———. 1977b. Logical form and conditions on rules. In *Proceedings of NELS VII*. Cambridge, Mass.: MIT Press.

———. 1978. Must Comp to Comp movement be stipulated? Paper presented at the annual meeting of the Linguistic Society of America, Boston. *Linguistic Inquiry* 10:719–725.

PARTEE, B. H. 1972. Opacity, coreference and pronouns. In *Semantics of natural language*, ed. D. Davidson and G. Harmon. Dordrecht: D. Reidel.

PETTIGREW, T. 1964. *A profile of the Negro American*. Princeton, N.J.: Van Nostrand.

PLANCK, M. 1949. Phantom problems in science. In *Scientific autobiography and other papers*. New York: Philosophical Library.

POPPER, K. 1963. The demarcation between science and metaphysics. In *Conjectures and refutations: The growth of scientific knowledge*. New York: Harper & Row.

POSTAL, P. 1972. The best theory. In *Goals of linguistic theory*, ed. S. Peters. Englewood Cliffs, N.J.: Prentice-Hall.

PULLUM, G. 1979. The nonexistence of the trace-binding algorithm. *Linguistic Inquiry* 10:356–362.

REINHART, T. 1976. The syntactic domain of anaphora. Doctoral dissertation, Massachusetts Institute of Technology.

REINHART, T. 1978. Syntactic domains for semantic rules. In *Formal semantics and pragmatics*, ed. F. Guenthner and S. J. Schmidt. Dordrecht: D. Reidel.

ROSENBAUM, P. S. 1967. *The grammar of English predicate complement constructions*. Cambridge, Mass.: MIT Press.

ROSS, J. 1967. Constraints on variables in syntax. Doctoral dissertation, Massachusetts Institute of Technology.

SELKIRK, E. O. 1972. The phrase phonology of English and French. Doctoral dissertation, Massachusetts Institute of Technology.

SIEGEL, D. 1973. Nonsources of unpassives. In *Syntax and semantics,* vol. 1, ed. J. Kimball. New York: Academic Press.

SIEGEL, D. 1974. Topics in English morphology. Doctoral dissertation, Massachusetts Institute of Technology.

Index